101
3-5 STUNTS

Leo Hand

ISBN: 1-58518-885-9
Library of Congress Control Number: 2003117100
Book layout and diagrams: Deborah Oldenburg
Cover design: Jeanne Hamilton
Front cover photo: Brian Bahr/Getty Images

Coaches Choice
PO Box 1828
Monterey, CA 93942
www.coacheschoice.com

Dedication

For my wife Mary and her father Don Kee Yazie, a Navajo Medicine Man, who spent much of his life praying, conducting religious ceremonies, healing his people, and ……. sitting in jail cells because it was illegal for Native Americans to practice their religions in the United States until the American Indian Religious Freedom Act became law in 1979.

This book is also dedicated to Leonard Peltier.

Acknowledgments

- Thanks to Tony Shaw for giving me the opportunity to coach in Texas.

- Thanks to Jim Murphy, Don Kloppenberg, and Will Shaw for all they taught me about defense at Long Beach City College.

- Thanks to the wonderful people of the Zuni and Navajo Nations who taught me much more than I taught them during the seven years I lived with them.

- Thanks to Joe Griffin for giving me one of the best coaching jobs in California.

- Thanks to all of the splendid young men whom I have been privileged to coach.

- Thanks to all of the great coaches whom I have been fortunate to have worked with and coached against.

- Thanks to Phil Johnson for all of his help and kind words.

- Thanks to Conrado Ronquillo, Joe Barba, and the maintenance crew at Irvin High School for all of their patience, kindness and help during this project.

- Thanks to Sam Snoddy for his assistance during this project.

- Thanks to the offspring whose ancestors endured the *Middle Chamber* and the *Long Walk* for all of the contributions that they have made to the greatest game of all.

- Thanks to Howard Wells and Ron Detinger for giving me the chance to coach at El Paso High School.

- Thanks to Knifewing, whose music inspired the words of this book.

- Thanks to Herman Masin, editor of *Scholastic Coach*, for all of his help and suggestions during the past 30 years.

- Thanks to Dr. James A Peterson for all of his help and encouragement.

Contents

Dedication. 3

Acknowledgments 4

Introduction 6

Chapter 1: Eleven Stunt Strategies that Win Games 9

Chapter 2: Basic Principles of Blitzing 17

Chapter 3: Zero Coverage Stunts. 20

Chapter 4: Cover 1 Stunts. 52

Chapter 5: Cover 3 Stunts. 101

Chapter 6: Cover 2 Zone Stunts 114

Chapter 7: Cover 2 Man Stunts 129

Chapter 8: Adapting 3-5 Stunt Tactics to Aceback and Empty Formations 139

Chapter 9: Defending the Option with the 3-5 Defense. 152

Chapter 10: A Synopsis of D-Line/Linebacker Base Responsibilities. 157

About the Author. 166

Introduction

What's in This Book for You

This book provides the reader with the following information:

- Eleven innovative stunt tactics that will enable your defense to actually attack the offense.
- An explanation of the assignments and techniques necessary to install football's newest defensive innovation–the fire zone blitz.
- 101 explosive stunts from a variety of man and zone pass coverages.
- A variety of examples showing how to adapt the 11 stunt strategies to aceback and empty formations.
- A thorough explanation of the assignments and techniques necessary to implement both man and zone pass coverages.
- An analysis of 3-5 option responsibilities.
- A synopsis of 3-5 d-line/linebacker base responsibilities.

Before We Begin

There are a few terms that will constantly be referred to throughout the text. Because different phrases and words can sometimes mean different things to different people, the following terms are defined and clarified as they are used in this book:

- **Strongside/weakside:** The strongside is toward the tight end and the weakside is toward the split end. Strong defenders (example: strong end) are aligned on the tight-end side, and weak defenders are aligned on the split-end side.
- Player position names are as illustrated in Figure Intro-1.

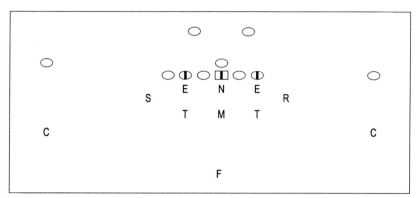

Figure Intro-1

- **Strong cornerback**—the cornerback who lines up opposite the flanker.
- **Weak cornerback**—the cornerback who lines up opposite the split end.
- **Rover (R)**—*the adjuster*. The defensive back/linebacker who lines up as an outside linebacker in an 8 technique toward the weak side.
- **Free Safety (FS)**—the safety who is aligned in centerfield.
- **Stud**—At the outside linebacker who lines up toward the strong side in an 8 technique.
- **Strong Tandem**—the inside linebacker who stacks behind the strong end.
- **Strong End**—the defensive lineman who lines up on the strong side in a 4 technique.
- **Nose**—the defensive lineman who lines up opposite the center in a 0 technique.
- **Mike**—the middle linebacker who lines up behind the nose.
- **Weak Tandem**—the inside linebacker who stacks behind the weak end.
- **Weak End**—the defensive lineman who lines up on the weak side in a 4 technique.

• Gap Responsibilities are lettered as illustrated in Figure Intro-2.

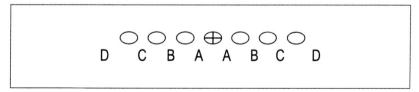

Figure Intro-2

- Alignments are numbered as illustrated in Figure Intro-3.

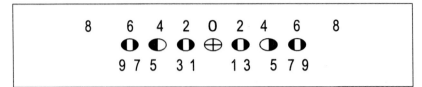

Figure Intro-3

- Receivers are numbered as illustrated in Figure Intro-4.

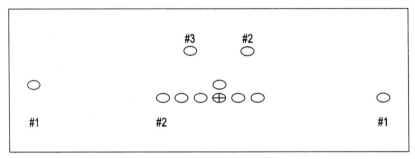

Figure Intro-4

1

Eleven Stunt Strategies that Win Games

Illusion Blitzes

The term blitz refers to a stunt that employs a 6-man pass rush. An illusion blitz is a specific type of blitz that gives the offense the *illusion* that the defense is "sending the house." When an illusion blitz is employed, seven or eight defenders attack the line of scrimmage at the snap. Against the run, these seven or eight defenders attempt to penetrate the gaps, control the line of scrimmage, force the ball carrier out of his intended course, and ultimately stop the play in the backfield. Against the pass, six of these defenders continue to rush the quarterback and the remaining one or two *fake pass rushers spy* the running back(s). Against the pass, illusion blitzes hold the offense accountable for blocking all seven or eight defenders aligned in the box, thereby limiting the number of receivers an offense can put into pass patterns and still safely protect it's the quarterback. Furthermore, illusion blitzes make pass protection a chaotic guessing game. Since the *spy* defenders are often defensive linemen, illusion blitzes not only cause offensive linemen to end up *blocking air*, they also eliminate many protection schemes that require offensive linemen to *double read* defensive alignments. Illusion blitzes are employed with zero coverage. Figure 1-1 illustrates an illusion blitz in which eight defenders are attacking the line of scrimmage at the snap, but as they recognize pass, two of the defenders *spy* the two running backs. If the running backs block instead of releasing for a pattern, the two *spy* defenders continue as *fake rushers*. It is vital that the *fake pass rushers* understand that spying the running backs takes precedence over *pretending* to rush the quarterback, otherwise, they may become vulnerable to delay pass routes or screen patterns.

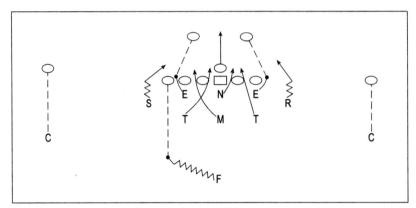

Figure 1-1

Blitzes

Illusion blitzes are usually called when the offense is expected to pass. Blitzes, on the other hand, are usually called in run situations. Many coaches use blitzes to pressure the offense from the edge and free up inside linebackers so that they can pursue the ball carrier from an inside-out position. Like illusion blitzes, blitzes are used with zero coverage. Figure 1-2 illustrates a blitz that sends the stud, rover, and mike linebackers.

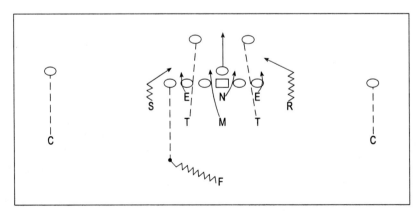

Figure 1-2

Illusion Dogs

The term *dog* refers to a stunt that employs a 5-man pass rush. Figure1-3 shows an example of an illusion dog in which the ends are spying the running backs. Illusion dogs are almost identical to illusion blitzes. The two differences between these two tactics are:

- Illusion dogs employ five-man pass rushes and illusion blitzes employ six-man pass rushes.
- Cover 1 is used with illusion dogs and zero coverage is used with illusion blitzes. Although illusion dogs put less pressure on a quarterback, many coaches feel more secure using them because their defense is afforded the luxury of a free safety who backs up the defenders in the box and plays centerfield versus the pass.

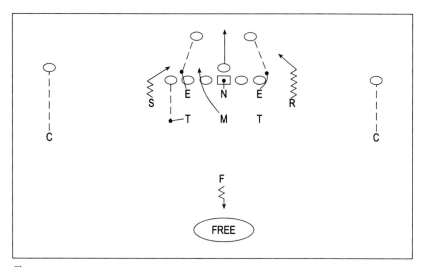

Figure 1-3

Dogs

Dogs and blitzes are like illusion dogs and illusion blitzes in their similarities and differences. Figure 1-4 shows an example of a dog that sends the mike and the weak tandem.

Fire Zone Blitzes

Fire zone blitzes are not really blitzes; they're actually dogs because they involve five-man pass rushes, and they're used with cover 1. However, since fire zone blitz has become the universal term used to describe this tactic, it will be used in this book. A fire zone blitz is a variation of an illusion dog. Unlike illusion dogs however, fire zone blitzes have three defenders drop off into the under coverage and combo-cover the tight end and two running backs versus pass. The areas that these three defenders drop off into will be referred to in this book as **Abel**, **Baker**, and **Charlie**. In addition to the all of the advantages gained by using illusion blitzes and dogs, fire zone blitzes often cause the quarterback to quickly dump the ball off to a *hot receiver* in a long passing situation. This frequently results in the offense failing to gain a first down. The specifics of the fire zone blitz will be discussed in a later chapter. Figure 1-5 shows an example of a common fire zone blitz that has the stud, mike and the weak end dropping into coverage.

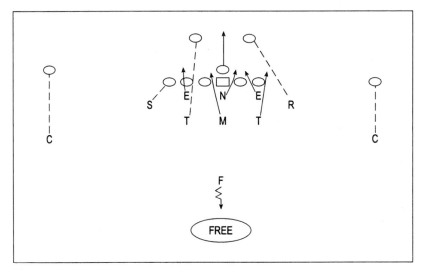

Figure 1-4

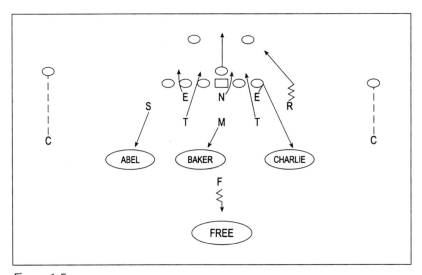

Figure 1-5

Hybrid Fire Zone Blitzes

This tactic combines a strongside fire zone concept with a weakside illusion. Figure 1-6 illustrates a hybrid fire zone blitz in which the stud and strong tandem drop off into coverage and combo-cover the tight end and strong halfback (similar to a fire zone **Abel-Baker** drop) while the weak end spies the weakside halfback.

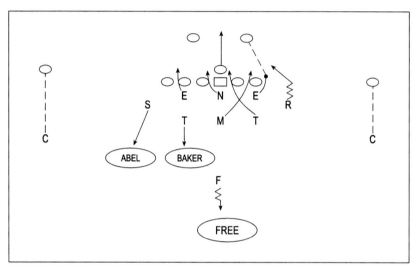

Figure 1-6

Old School Zone Blitzes

Back when Tom Bass was coaching in the NFL, he frequently blitzed linebackers and dropped defensive linemen into coverage. Unlike today's fire zone blitz, the pass coverage Coach Bass used to implement this tactic was a two- or three-deep zone. Figure 1-7 shows an *old school* zone blitz using a variation of cover 3 in which the nose drops off into coverage.

Overloads

Overloads attempt to get more pass rushers on one side of the ball than available pass blockers. Both strongside and weakside overloads are easily attainable using the 3-5 by having a defensive lineman or linebacker employ a delayed pass rush. Figure 1-8 shows a weakside overload that is created by a delayed pass rush by the mike. This delayed rush by mike puts the defense in the dilemma of trying to block four pass rushers (illusion of five rushers) with three pass blockers.

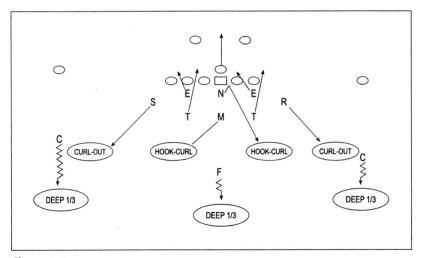

Figure 1-7

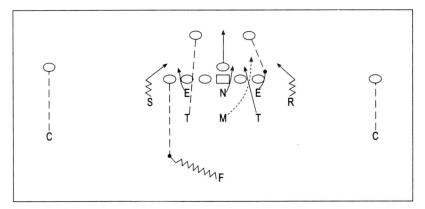

Figure 1-8

Line Twists

Line twists have always been an effective weapon versus both pass and run. Line twists can occur as the ball is being snapped, or they can be implemented as delayed reactions to pass. Figure 1-9 illustrates a line twist that occurs as the ball is snapped. This line twist is shown being used in conjunction with cover 3.

Secondary Blitzes

Secondary blitzes and fake secondary blitzes are powerful multifaceted weapons that can easily be incorporated into a multitude of 3-5 blitz and illusion blitz schemes. Figure 1-10 shows a free safety blitz that is incorporated into an illusion blitz scheme.

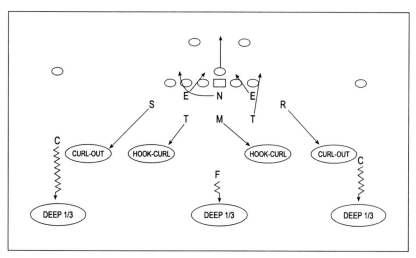

Figure 1-9

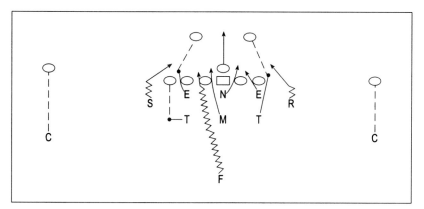

Figure 1-10

Twin Stunts

Whenever two players stunt through the same gap, it is referred to as a *twin stunt*. Defensive backs, linebackers, or linemen can be used to create twin stunts. Figure 1-11 shows a twin stunt that is achieved by the nose delay rushing through the weakside B gap behind the weak end. This is an unusual tactic. Since few offensive teams ever see this type of stunt, it is often very effective. Twin stunts are usually called in passing situations.

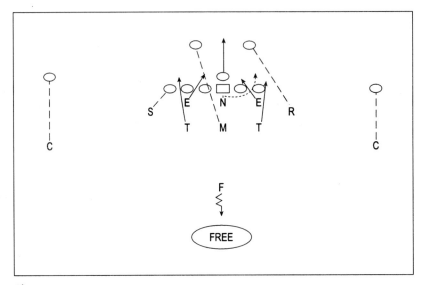

Figure 1-11

2

Basic Principles of Blitzing

- If a player blitzes infrequently, using it as an element of surprise, it's important that disguises his intention.

- If a player frequently blitzes, disguising his intention may not be as important because he may want to occasionally give the offense a false key by *showing blitz* but then *playing straight* at the snap of the ball. Whichever strategy he decides to use, it is important that the does not establish a pattern that can be exploited.

- A player's eyes are one of his most important tools when blitzing. To be an effective blitzer, a player must be able to see (on the run) the keys that that will lead him to the ball. Seeing these keys is the first step in being able to read and react to them.

- Unless the blitz is a delayed reaction to a pass, it is critical that the blitzer is moving, attacking, and penetrating the line of scrimmage at the snap of the ball.

- A blitzer must keep his feet moving at all times. This is especially important when he becomes engaged with a blocker.

- A blitzing player should use his quickness in an attempt to avoid blockers.

- If the play is a pass, and the blitzer becomes engaged with a blocker, he should keep his hands inside of the blocker's hands and try to maintain separation from the blocker. He should not look at the passer too soon, or he may lose sight of the blocker. The blitzer must first defeat the blocker before he can sack the quarterback. While a blitzer should have a predetermined pass rush move in mind, he should be ready to change his move according to the circumstances. A blitzer needs to take what the blocker gives him and make his move at the appropriate time. Remember that if a blitzing player makes his pass rush move too soon, the blocker will have time to recover. On the other hand, if he makes his move too late, he will probably be too close to the blocker, thereby enabling the blocker to get into the blitzer's body and nullify his charge. If possible, the blitzer should try to get the blocker turned one way and then make his move in the opposite direction. The blitzing player should also use his forward momentum to manipulate the blocker's momentum. If the blocker's momentum is back, the blitzer should attack him with a power move and knock him backwards. If his momentum is forward, the blitzer can use a move that pulls him forward and destroys his balance. A blitzing player should never leave his feet to bat a ball down. He should get his hands up as the quarterback begins his throwing motion, but continue his charge toward the quarterback. Too often, when a defender jumps up to bat a pass down, the quarterback will duck under, elude the defender, and scramble out of the pocket.

- If the play is a run, a blitzer should react to his keys and the pressure of blocks as he normally would if he were employing a read technique. Since a blitzer has forward momentum to his advantage, he should use his hands rather than his forearm when attacking a blocker. A blitzing player should maintain separation from blockers and not let them get into his legs. If possible, blitzers should try to make the blocker miss.

- When blitzing, a player should keep his body under control at all times, try to maintain a low center of gravity, and provide as small a target as possible for the blockers.

- Blitzers need to study their opponents' game films carefully. They should know how their potential blockers react and what techniques they favor. It helps to know the strengths and weaknesses of the opponent.

- A blitzer should also study his opponent's eyes as he's getting set at the line of scrimmage. The blocker's eyes will often tell a blitzer where he's going. Studying the pressure that the blocker puts on his down hand when he gets into his stance will also frequently give a pass/run or a directional key.

- Blitzers who study the scouting report will increase their knowledge of the opponents' formation, down-and-distance, and field-position tendencies. They should use this information to anticipate, but never to guess.

- All players should gang tackle and try to strip the ball out of the ball carrier's arm. Players should never take for granted that a running back or quarterback has been downed. If they arrive at a pile late, they should be on the alert for a loose ball.

- Players must maintain total intensity from the time the ball is snapped until the whistle is blown.

- Before the snap, a blitzer should anticipate potential blockers and be prepared to react to those blockers as he penetrates the line.

- On plays directed toward a blitzer's side of the field, he should make the tackle. On plays directed away from him, he should take the proper angle of pursuit and be in on the tackle. Players should always pursue relentlessly. Remember that if a player is not within five yards of the ball when the whistle blows that he is probably loafing.

- If the backfield action does not indicate flow, a blitzer should protect his gap until he finds the ball. He should never guess.

- If a player is assigned to *spy* (cover a back) when he's blitzing, he should expect that the back will first block and then run a delayed route. He cannot be fooled. Remind him that he must cover the back, no matter what the back does until the whistle blows.

- The ball is the blitzer's trigger. When the ball is snapped, *he's gone!* He should not listen to an opponent's cadence; they're not talking to him!

- Players should not rely upon the lines that are marked on the field. The ball, not the lines, establishes the line of scrimmage.

3

Zero Coverage Stunts

When zero coverage is employed, there will be no free safeties. The three defensive backs will be assigned to guard the tight end and two wide receivers man-to-man, and two defenders in the box will be assigned to cover the two running backs. Zero coverage is used with blitzes and illusion blitzes.

The strength of zero coverage is that it has six defenders (blitz scheme) or seven/eight defenders (illusion blitz scheme) attacking gaps and penetrating the line of scrimmage. Its weakness is that all secondary defenders are locked on receivers and none are keying the ball; therefore, if a runner breaks the line of scrimmage or a defensive back gets beat deep, there is a good chance that a touchdown will result. Despite this weakness, zero coverage can cause an offense a lot of problems, especially when the defenders in the box have some "quicks," and the defensive backs are skillful man-to-man pass defenders.

Secondary Man-Man Techniques for Zero Coverage

Stance & Alignment

A defensive secondary player should:

- Align himself with an inside shade on the receiver, approximately seven yards deep.

- Set up with a narrow base, feet inside of his armpits, outside foot up (toe-heel relationship).
- Keep his weight on his front foot.
- Keep his knees bent and his hips lowered.
- Slightly round his back with his head and shoulders over his front foot (nose over the toes).
- Allow his arms to hang loose.
- See both the receiver and quarterback with his peripheral vision.

Backpedal

A defensive secondary player should:

- Maintain inside leverage on the receiver.
- Keep a good forward lean as he backpedals (chin down and nose over the toes).
- Push off his front foot and take his first step with his back foot. He should never step forward or lift a foot and set it back down in the same place.
- Keep his weight on the balls of his feet.
- Reach back with each step and pull his weight over his feet.
- Keep his feet close to the ground during the backpedal.
- Not over-stride; take small-to-medium steps.
- Keep his arms bent at a 90-degree angles—relaxed, but pumping vigorously.
- Maintain a proper cushion. When the receiver gets 10 yards downfield, the defender should be 15 yards deep. When the receiver is 15 yards downfield, the defenders should be 18 yards deep.
- Remember and anticipate that 3-step routes are usually thrown five to seven yards downfield (the exception being the fade); 5-step patterns are thrown 8-15 yards downfield; and 7-step routes are usually thrown 18+ yards downfield.
- Be aware of a receiver's split. Wide splits often indicate inside routes; tight splits often indicate outside routes.
- Keep his shoulders parallel to the line and not let the receiver turn him.
- Mirror the receiver's movements while keeping his own outside shoulder on the receiver's inside shoulder. He must not let the receiver get head up with him
- Control the speed of his backpedal. When the receiver makes his break, the defender must be under control and able to gather and break quickly in the direction of the break.

- Concentrate on the base of the receiver's numbers until he makes his final break.
- Anticipate a break when the receiver changes his forward lean, begins to chop his feet, or begins to widen his base.
- Honor all inside fakes.
- Not backpedal at the snap if aligned on a tight end. Be ready to jump a flat or crossing route. If the tight end goes vertical, the defender must work to an inside-leverage position.
- Remember that "if the receiver gets even (with the defender), he's leavin'." Whenever a receiver gets too close, the defender must turn and run with him, keeping his body between the receiver and the ball. He must not allow separation to occur. As he's running with the receiver, he can try to disrupt the receiver's strides by slapping at his near hand and wrist.

Plant & Drive

- When the receiver makes his final break, the defensive back should drop his shoulder in the direction of the receiver's break and explode in that direction. He must make his break parallel to the receiver's break, and quickly close the cushion.
- The defender must not lose concentration on the receiver. He should not look for the ball until he's closed his cushion and he sees the receiver look for the ball.
- If the receiver tries to change direction after the defender has begun his drive, the defensive player should be in a position so that the receiver will have to make contact with him in order to change directions.

Playing the Ball

A defensive secondary player should:

- Attack the ball at its highest point.
- Play the ball, not the receiver, when the ball is to his inside and the receiver is outside of him.
- Play the ball through the receiver's up field shoulder when the receiver is between him and the ball. He should never cut in front of the receiver to make an interception unless he is sure that he can get two hands on the ball.
- Try to catch the ball or break up a pass with two hands, not one.
- Always knock the ball toward the ground, never up in the air.
- Try to strip the ball if the receiver catches the pass.
- Head to the nearest sideline after intercepting a pass.
- Always look the ball into his hands and protect it after he catches it.

Adjusting Zero Coverage to Offensive Formations

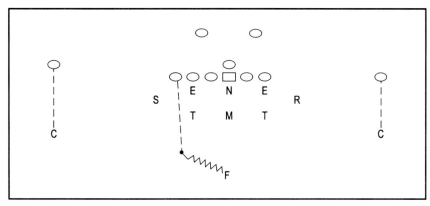

Figure 3-1a

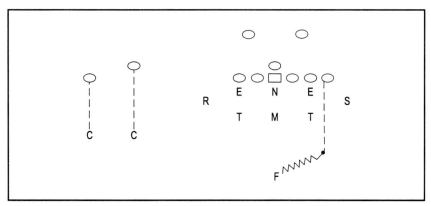

Figure 3-1b

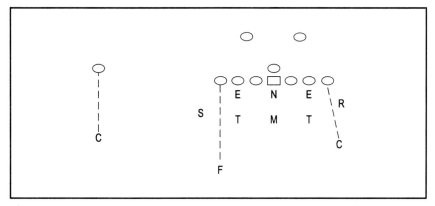

Figure 3-1c

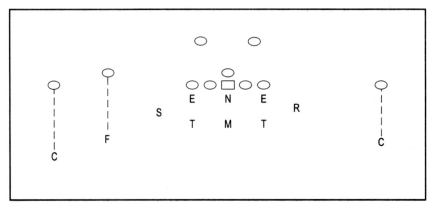

Figure 3-1d

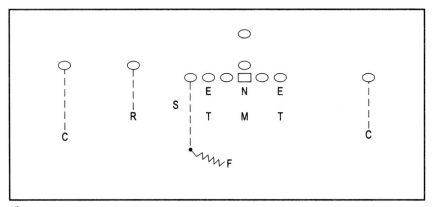

Figure 3-1e

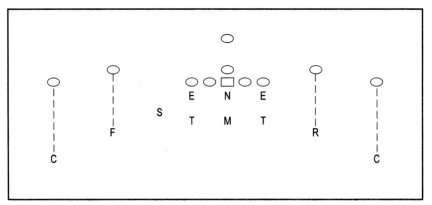

Figure 3-1f

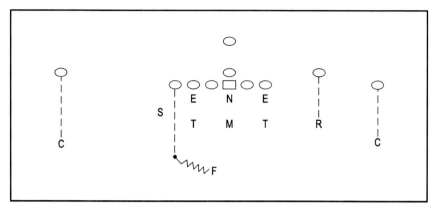

Figure 3-1g

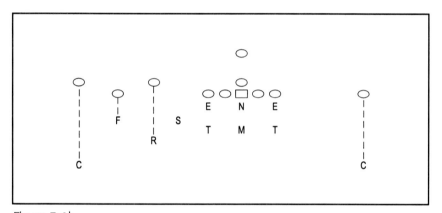

Figure 3-1h

STUNT #1

STUNT DESCRIPTION: This is an *illusion blitz*.

SECONDARY COVERAGE: Zero coverage disguised as cover 1. Both tandems fake blitz into the C gaps and spy the running backs.

STUD: Creeps toward the line of scrimmage during cadence and rushes from the edge. Contains the quarterback and strongside run. Chases weakside run.

STRONG END: Attacks the near shoulder of the offensive guard. Controls the B gap.

STRONG TANDEM: Stunts through the outside shoulder of the offensive tackle. Secures the C gap. Spies the near back versus pass.

NOSE: Slants to the strongside A gap.

MIKE: Stunts to the weakside A gap.

WEAK END: Attacks the near shoulder of the offensive guard. Controls the B gap.

WEAK TANDEM: Stunts through the outside shoulder of the offensive tackle. Secures the C gap versus run and spies the near back versus pass.

ROVER: Creeps toward the line of scrimmage during cadence and rushes from the edge. Contains the quarterback and weakside run. Chases strongside run.

FREE SAFETY: Covers the tight end. Disguises his assignment as cover 1.

STRONG CORNER: Covers the flanker (inside technique).

WEAK CORNER: Covers the split end (inside technique).

STUNT #2

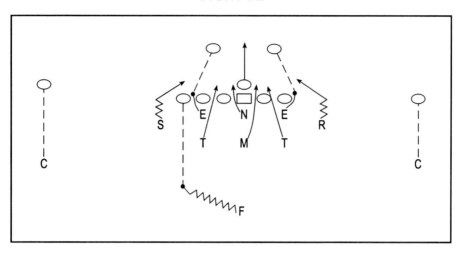

STUNT DESCRIPTION: This is an *illusion blitz*.

SECONDARY COVERAGE: Zero coverage disguised as cover 1. Ends slant into the C gaps and spy the running backs.

STUD: Creeps toward the line of scrimmage during cadence and rushes from the edge. Contains the quarterback and strongside run. Chases weakside run.

STRONG END: Slants to the C gap. Spies the near back versus pass.

STRONG TANDEM: Stunts through the outside shoulder of the offensive guard and secures the B gap.

NOSE: Slants to the strongside A gap.

MIKE: Stunts to the weakside A gap.

WEAK END: Slants to the C gap. Spies the near back versus pass.

WEAK TANDEM: Stunts through the outside shoulder of the offensive guard and secures the B gap.

ROVER: Creeps toward the line of scrimmage during cadence and rushes from the edge. Contains the quarterback and weakside run. Chases strongside run.

FREE SAFETY: Covers the tight end. Disguises his assignment as cover 1.

STRONG CORNER: Covers the flanker (inside technique).

WEAK CORNER: Covers the split end (inside technique).

STUNT #3

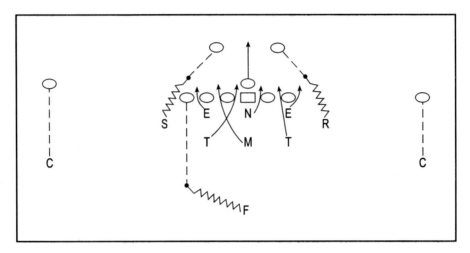

STUNT DESCRIPTION: This is an *illusion blitz*.

SECONDARY COVERAGE: Zero coverage disguised as cover 1. Stud and Rover give impression they are rushing from the edge and spy the running backs.

STUD: Creeps toward the line of scrimmage during cadence and gives the impression he is rushing from the edge. Contains strongside run and chases weakside run. Spies the near back versus pass.

STRONG END: Slants to the C gap. Contains the quarterback versus pass.

STRONG TANDEM: Stunts through the strongside A gap. Because Mike goes first, he makes his first step parallel to the line with his right foot.

NOSE: Slants to the weakside A gap.

MIKE: Stunts to the strongside B gap. He goes first. He will therefore step directly at his landmark as the ball is snapped.

WEAK END: Slants to the C gap. Contains the quarterback versus pass.

WEAK TANDEM: Stunts through the inside shoulder of the offensive guard and secures the B gap.

ROVER: Creeps toward the line of scrimmage during cadence and gives impression he is rushing from the edge. Contains weakside run and chases strongside run. Spies the near back versus pass.

FREE SAFETY: Covers the tight end. Disguises his assignment as cover 1.

STRONG CORNER: Covers the flanker (inside technique).

WEAK CORNER: Covers the split end (inside technique).

STUNT DESCRIPTION: This is an *illusion blitz*.

SECONDARY COVERAGE: Zero coverage disguised as cover 1. The strong Tandem and weak end control C gaps versus run and spy the running backs versus pass.

STUD: Creeps toward the line of scrimmage during cadence and rushes from the edge. Contains the quarterback and strongside run. Chases weakside run.

STRONG END: Attacks the near shoulder of the offensive guard and controls the C gap.

STRONG TANDEM: Stunts through the outside shoulder of the offensive tackle, secures the C gap versus run, and spies the near back versus pass.

NOSE: Slants to the strongside A gap.

MIKE: Stunts to the weakside B gap. The Weak Tandem goes first. He therefore makes his first step parallel to the line with his right foot.

WEAK END: Slants outside and controls the C gap. Spies the near back versus pass.

WEAK TANDEM: Blitzes through the weakside A gap. He goes first. He therefore makes his first step directly at his landmark.

ROVER: Creeps toward the line of scrimmage during cadence and rushes from the edge. Contains the quarterback and weakside run. Chases strongside run.

FREE SAFETY: Covers the tight end. Disguises his assignment as cover 1.

STRONG CORNER: Covers the flanker (inside technique).

WEAK CORNER: Covers the split end (inside technique).

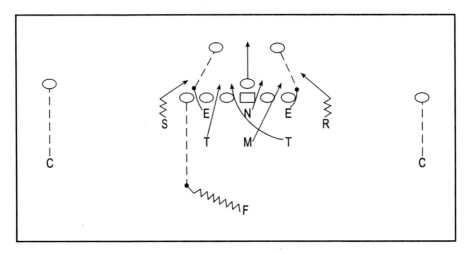

STUNT DESCRIPTION: This is an *illusion blitz*.

SECONDARY COVERAGE: Zero coverage disguised as cover 1. Both ends control the C gaps versus run and spy the running backs versus pass.

STUD: Creeps toward the line of scrimmage during cadence and rushes from the edge. Contains the quarterback and strongside run. Chases weakside run.

STRONG END: Slants to the C gap. Spies the near back versus pass.

STRONG TANDEM: Stunts through the near shoulder of the offensive guard and secures the B gap.

NOSE: Slants to the weakside A gap.

MIKE: Blitzes through the weakside B gap. He goes first.

WEAK END: Slants outside and controls the C gap. Spies the near back versus pass.

WEAK TANDEM: Blitzes through the strongside A gap. Mike goes first; he therefore makes his first step parallel to the line with his left foot.

ROVER: Creeps toward the line of scrimmage during the quarterback cadence and rushes from the edge. Contains the quarterback and weakside run. Chases strongside run.

FREE SAFETY: Covers the tight end. Disguises his assignment as cover 1.

STRONG CORNER: Covers the flanker (inside technique).

WEAK CORNER: Covers the split end (inside technique).

STUNT DESCRIPTION: This is a *blitz*.

SECONDARY COVERAGE: Zero coverage disguised as cover 1. The Stud and Rover play base technique versus run and cover the running backs versus pass.

STUD: Plays 8 technique versus run. Covers the near back versus pass.

STRONG END: Slants to the C gap. Contains the quarterback versus pass.

STRONG TANDEM: Blitzes through the weakside A gap. Mike goes first; he therefore makes his first step parallel to the line with his right foot.

NOSE: Slants to the strongside A gap.

MIKE: Blitzes through the strongside B gap. He goes first.

WEAK END: Attacks the near shoulder of the offensive guard and secures the B gap.

WEAK TANDEM: Stunts toward the outside shoulder of the offensive tackle. Secures the C gap versus run and contains the quarterback versus pass.

ROVER: Plays 8 technique versus run. Covers the near back versus pass.

FREE SAFETY: Covers the tight end. Disguises his assignment as cover 1.

STRONG CORNER: Covers the flanker (inside technique).

WEAK CORNER: Covers the split end (inside technique).

STUNT #7

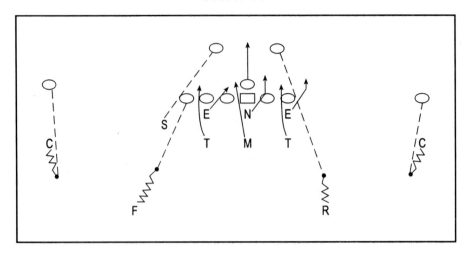

STUNT DESCRIPTION: This is a *blitz*.

SECONDARY COVERAGE: Zero coverage disguised as cover 2. The Stud and Rover play base technique versus run and cover the running backs versus pass.

STUD: Plays 8 technique versus run. Covers the near back versus pass.

STRONG END: Attacks the near shoulder of the offensive guard and secures the B gap.

STRONG TANDEM: Stunts toward the outside shoulder of the offensive tackle. Secures the C gap versus run and contains the quarterback versus pass.

NOSE: Slants to the weakside A gap.

MIKE: Blitzes through the strongside A gap.

WEAK END: Slants outside. Controls the C gap versus run and contains the quarterback versus pass.

WEAK TANDEM: Blitzes through the weakside B gap.

ROVER: Plays 8 technique versus run. Covers the near back versus pass. Disguises his assignment as cover 2.

FREE SAFETY: Covers the tight end. Disguises his assignment as Cover 2.

STRONG CORNER: Covers the flanker (inside technique). Disguises his assignment as cover 2.

WEAK CORNER: Covers the split end (inside technique). Disguises his assignment as cover 2.

STUNT #8

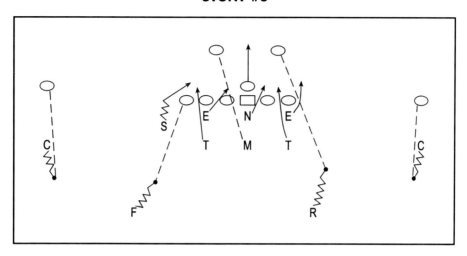

STUNT DESCRIPTION: This is a *dog*.

SECONDARY COVERAGE: Zero coverage disguised as cover 2. The Mike and Rover play base technique versus run and cover the running backs versus pass.

STUD: Creeps toward the line of scrimmage during cadence and rushes from the edge. Contains the quarterback and strongside run. Chases weakside run.

STRONG END: Attacks the near shoulder of the offensive guard and secures the B gap.

STRONG TANDEM: Stunts toward the outside shoulder of the offensive tackle and secures the C gap.

NOSE: Slants to the weakside A gap.

MIKE: Plays base technique versus run. Covers the near back versus pass.

WEAK END: Slants outside. Controls the C gap versus run and contains the quarterback versus pass.

WEAK TANDEM: Blitzes through the weakside B gap.

ROVER: Plays 8 technique versus run. Covers the near back versus pass. Disguises his assignment as cover 2.

FREE SAFETY: Covers the tight end. Disguises his assignment as cover 2.

STRONG CORNER: Covers the flanker (inside technique). Disguises his assignment as cover 2.

WEAK CORNER: Covers the split end (inside technique). Disguises his assignment as cover 2.

STUNT #9

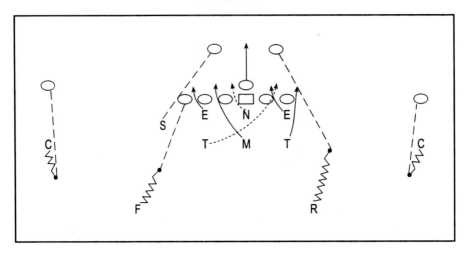

STUNT DESCRIPTION: This is a *blitz* that employs a *delayed linebacker blitz*.

SECONDARY COVERAGE: Zero coverage disguised as cover 2. The Stud and Rover play base technique versus run and cover the running backs versus pass.

STUD: Plays 8 technique versus run. Covers the near back versus pass.

STRONG END: Slants outside. Controls the C gap versus run. Contains the quarterback versus pass.

STRONG TANDEM: Plays base technique versus run. Delay blitzes through the weakside B gap versus pass.

NOSE: Plays 0 technique versus run. Slants into the strong A gap versus pass.

MIKE: Blitzes through the strongside B gap.

WEAK END: Slants into the B gap. It is vital that he gains quick penetration.

WEAK TANDEM: Stunts toward the outside shoulder of the offensive tackle. Secures the C gap versus run and contains the quarterback versus pass.

ROVER: Plays 8 technique versus run Covers the near back versus pass. Disguises his assignment as cover 2.

FREE SAFETY: Covers the tight end. Disguises his assignment as cover 2.

STRONG CORNER: Covers the flanker (inside technique). Disguises his assignment as cover 2.

WEAK CORNER: Covers the split end (inside technique). Disguises his assignment as cover 2.

STUNT #10

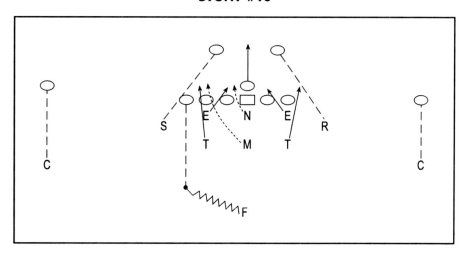

STUNT DESCRIPTION: This is a *blitz* that employs a *twin stunt* via a *delayed linebacker blitz* that achieves a *strongside overload*.

SECONDARY COVERAGE: Zero coverage disguised as cover 1. The Stud and Rover play base technique versus run and cover the running backs versus pass.

STUD: Plays 8 technique versus run. Covers the near back versus pass.

STRONG END: Slants to the B gap. It is imperative that he gains quick penetration through this gap.

STRONG TANDEM: Blitzes through the outside shoulder of the offensive tackle. Secures the C gap versus run and contains the quarterback versus pass.

NOSE: Plays 0 technique versus run. Slants into the strongside A gap versus pass.

MIKE: Plays base technique versus run. Delay blitzes through the strongside B gap versus pass.

WEAK END: Attacks the near shoulder of the offensive guard and secures the B gap.

WEAK TANDEM: Stunts toward the outside shoulder of the offensive tackle. Secures the C gap versus run and contains the quarterback versus pass.

ROVER: Plays 8 technique versus run. Covers the near back versus pass.

FREE SAFETY: Covers the tight end. Disguises his assignment as cover 1.

STRONG CORNER: Covers the flanker (inside technique).

WEAK CORNER: Covers the split end (inside technique).

STUNT #11

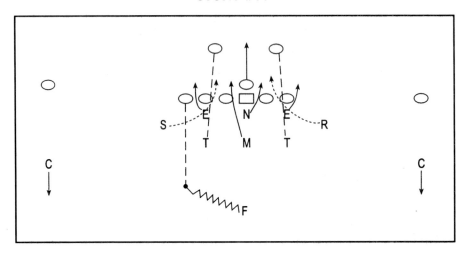

STUNT DESCRIPTION: This is a *blitz* that features two *delayed linebacker blitzes*.

SECONDARY COVERAGE: Zero coverage disguised as cover 1. The Tandems cover the near backs. The Stud and Rover play base technique versus run and delay blitz versus pass.

STUD: Plays 8 technique versus run. Delay blitz through the strongside B gap versus pass.

STRONG END: Slants to the C gap. Contains the quarterback versus pass.

STRONG TANDEM: Plays base technique versus run. Cover the near back versus pass.

NOSE: Slants to the weakside A gap.

MIKE: Blitzes through the strongside A gap.

WEAK END: Slants to the C gap. Contains the quarterback versus pass.

WEAK TANDEM: Plays base technique versus run. Covers the near back versus pass

ROVER: Plays 8 technique versus run. Delay blitzes through the weakside B gap versus pass.

FREE SAFETY: Covers the tight end. Disguises his assignment as cover 1.

STRONG CORNER: Covers the flanker (inside technique).

WEAK CORNER: Covers the split end (inside technique).

STUNT #12

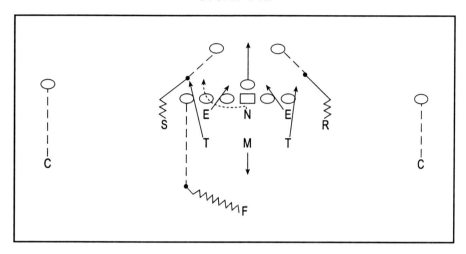

STUNT DESCRIPTION: This is an *illusion dog* that provides the defense with a *strongside twin stunt* and keeps Mike free to back up the defenders who penetrate the gaps.

SECONDARY COVERAGE: Zero coverage disguised as over 1. The Stud and Rover spy the running backs.

STUD: Creeps toward the line of scrimmage during cadence and rushes from the edge. Contains strongside run and chases weakside run. Spies the near back versus pass

STRONG END: Slants to the B gap. It is imperative that he quickly gains penetration through this gap.

STRONG TANDEM: Blitzes through the C gap. Contains the quarterback versus pass.

NOSE: Plays 0 technique versus run. Loops through the strongside B gap versus pass.

MIKE: Plays base technique versus run. Drops into the hole versus pass.

WEAK END: Attacks the near shoulder of the offensive guard and controls the B gap.

WEAK TANDEM: Stunts through the outside shoulder of the offensive tackle. Controls the C gap versus run and contains the quarterback versus pass.

ROVER: Creeps toward the line of scrimmage during cadence and rushes from the edge. Contains strongside run and chases weakside run. Spies the near back versus pass.

FREE SAFETY: Covers the tight end. Disguises his assignment as cover 1.

STRONG CORNER: Covers the flanker (inside technique).

WEAK CORNER: Covers the split end (inside technique).

STUNT #13

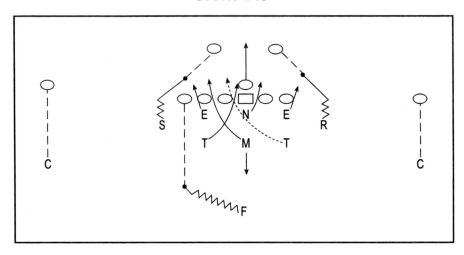

STUNT DESCRIPTION: This is a *blitz* that provides the defense with a *twin stunt* that creates a *strongside overload*.

SECONDARY COVERAGE: Zero coverage disguised as cover 1. The Stud and Rover spy the running backs and the weak Tandem delay blitzes through the strongside A gap.

STUD: Creeps toward the line of scrimmage during cadence and rushes from the edge. Contains strongside run and chases weakside run. Spies the near back versus pass.

STRONG END: Slants into and secures the C gap versus run. Contains the quarterback versus pass.

STRONG TANDEM: Blitzes through the strongside A gap. Mike goes first.

NOSE: Slants into and controls the weakside A gap.

MIKE: Blitzes through the strongside B gap. He goes first.

WEAK END: Slants into and secures the C gap versus run and contains the quarterback versus pass.

WEAK TANDEM: Plays base technique versus run. Delay blitzes through the strongside A gap versus pass.

ROVER: Creeps toward the line of scrimmageduring cadence and rushes from the edge. Contains strongside run and chases weakside run. Spies the near back versus pass.

FREE SAFETY: Covers the tight end. Disguises his assignment as cover 1.

STRONG CORNER: Covers the flanker (inside technique).

WEAK CORNER: Covers the split end (inside technique).

STUNT #14

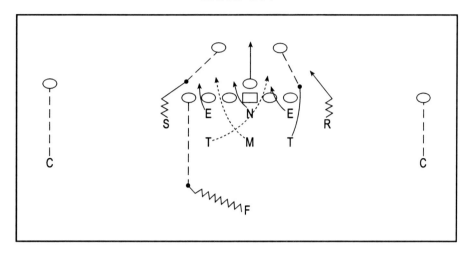

STUNT DESCRIPTION: This is a *blitz* that provides the defense with two *delayed linebacker blitzes*.

SECONDARY COVERAGE: Zero coverage disguised as cover 1. The Stud and the weak Tandem spy the running backs and the strong Tandem and Mike employ delayed blitzes.

STUD: Creeps toward the line of scrimmage during cadence and rushes from the edge. Contains strongside run and chases weakside run. Spies the near back versus pass.

STRONG END: Slants into and secures the C gap versus run and contains the quarterback versus pass.

STRONG TANDEM: Plays base technique versus run. Delay blitzes through the weakside A gap versus pass. Mike goes first.

NOSE: Slants into and controls the strongside A gap.

MIKE: Plays base technique versus run. Delay blitzes through the strongside B gap versus pass. He goes first.

WEAK END: Attacks the near shoulder of the offensive guard and controls the B gap.

WEAK TANDEM: Stunts into and secures the C gap versus run. Spies the near back versus pass.

ROVER: Creeps toward the line of scrimmage during cadence and rushes from the edge. Contains the quarterback and strongside run. Chases weakside run.

FREE SAFETY: Covers the tight end. Disguises his assignment as cover 1.

STRONG CORNER: Covers the flanker (inside technique).

WEAK CORNER: Covers the split end (inside technique).

STUNT #15

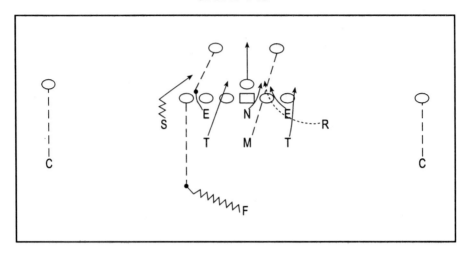

STUNT DESCRIPTION: This is a *blitz* that provides the defense with a *weakside overload* pass rush.

SECONDARY COVERAGE: Zero coverage disguised as cover 1. The strong end and Mike cover the running backs.

STUD: Creeps toward the line of scrimmage during cadence and rushes from the edge. Contains the quarterback and strongside run. Chases weakside run.

STRONG END: Slants into and secures the C gap versus run and spies the near back versus pass.

STRONG TANDEM: Stunts through the outside shoulder of the offensive guard and secures the B gap.

NOSE: Slants into and controls the weakside A gap.

MIKE: Plays base technique versus run. Covers the weak back versus pass.

WEAK END: Slants through the B gap. It is vital that he gains quick penetration through this gap.

WEAK TANDEM: Stunts through the outside shoulder of the offensive tackle. Secures the C gap versus run and contains the quarterback versus pass.

ROVER: Plays 8 technique versus run. Delay blitzes through the weakside B gap versus pass.

FREE SAFETY: Covers the tight end. Disguises his assignment as cover 1.

STRONG CORNER: Covers the flanker (inside technique).

WEAK CORNER: Covers the split end (inside technique).

STUNT #16

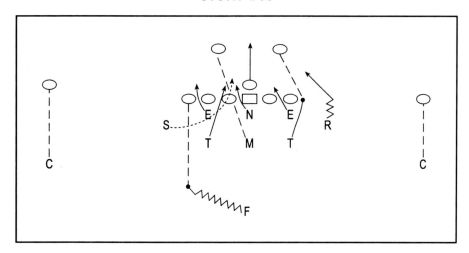

STUNT DESCRIPTION: This is a *blitz* that provides the defense with a *strongside overload* pass rush.

SECONDARY COVERAGE: Zero coverage disguised as cover 1. The weak Tandem and Mike cover the running backs.

STUD: Plays 8 technique versus run. Delay blitzes through the strongside B gap versus pass.

STRONG END: Slants into and secures the C gap versus run and contains the quarterback versus pass.

STRONG TANDEM: Blitzes through the B gap.

NOSE: Slants into and controls the strongside A gap.

MIKE: Plays base technique versus run. Covers the strong back versus pass.

WEAK END: Attacks the near shoulder of the offensive guard and controls the B gap.

WEAK TANDEM: Stunts through the outside shoulder of the offensive tackle. Secures the C gap versus run and spies the near back versus pass.

ROVER: Creeps toward the line of scrimmage during cadence and rushes from the edge. Contains the quarterback and weakside run. Chases strongside run.

FREE SAFETY: Covers the tight end. Disguises his assignment as cover 1.

STRONG CORNER: Covers the flanker (inside technique).

WEAK CORNER: Covers the split end (inside technique).

STUNT #17

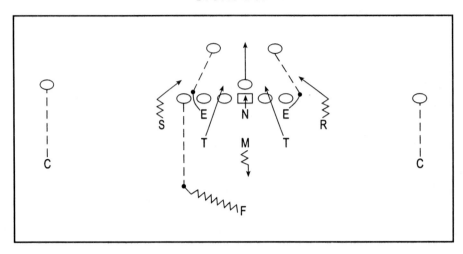

STUNT DESCRIPTION: This is an *illusion dog* that gives the *illusion* of a seven-man pass rush and keeps Mike free to back up the defenders who penetrate the gaps.

SECONDARY COVERAGE: Zero coverage disguised as cover 1. Ends spy the running backs.

STUD: Creeps toward the line of scrimmage during cadence and rushes from the edge. Contains the quarterback and strongside run. Chases weakside run.

STRONG END: Slants into and controls the C gap. Spies the near back versus pass.

STRONG TANDEM: Stunts through the outside shoulder of the offensive guard and controls the B gap.

NOSE: Plays 0 technique.

MIKE: Plays base technique versus run. Drops to the hole versus pass.

WEAK END: Slants into and controls the C gap. Spies the near back versus pass.

WEAK TANDEM: Stunts through the outside shoulder of the offensive guard and controls the B gap.

ROVER: Creeps toward the line of scrimmage during cadence and rushes from the edge. Contains the quarterback and weakside run. Chases strongside run.

FREE SAFETY: Covers the tight end. Disguises his assignment as cover 1.

STRONG CORNER: Covers the flanker (inside technique).

WEAK CORNER: Covers the split end (inside technique).

STUNT #18

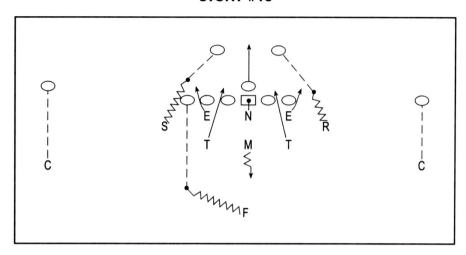

STUNT DESCRIPTION: This is an *illusion dog* that gives the *illusion* of a seven-man pass rush and keeps Mike free to back up the defenders who penetrate the gaps.

SECONDARY COVERAGE: Zero coverage disguised as cover 1. The Stud and Rover spy the running backs.

STUD: Creeps toward the line of scrimmage during cadence and rushes from the edge. Contains strongside run, chases weakside run, and spies the near back versus pass.

STRONG END: Slants into and secures the C gap versus run and contains the quarterback versus pass.

STRONG TANDEM: Stunts through the outside shoulder of the offensive guard and controls the B gap.

NOSE: Plays 0 technique.

MIKE: Plays base technique versus run. Drops to the hole versus pass.

WEAK END: Slants into and secures the C gap versus run and contains the quarterback versus pass.

WEAK TANDEM: Stunts through the outside shoulder of the offensive guard and controls the B gap.

ROVER: Creeps toward the line of scrimmage during cadence and rushes from the edge. Contains weak side run, chases strong side run, and spies the near back versus pass.

FREE SAFETY: Covers the tight end. Disguises his assignment as cover 1.

STRONG CORNER: Covers the flanker (inside technique).

WEAK CORNER: Covers the split end (inside technique).

STUNT #19

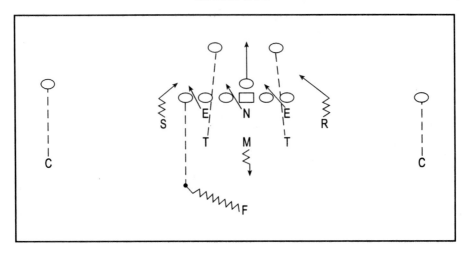

STUNT DESCRIPTION: This is a *dog* that provides the defense with a strongside line slant and excellent pressure from the edge. It also frees the Tandems and Mike to assist in run pursuit.

SECONDARY COVERAGE: Zero coverage disguised as cover 1. Tandems cover the running backs.

STUD: Creeps toward the line of scrimmage during cadence and rushes from the edge. Contains the quarterback and strongside run. Chases weakside run.

STRONG END: Slants into and controls the C gap.

STRONG TANDEM: Plays base technique versus run. Covers the near back versus pass.

NOSE: Plays 0 technique.

MIKE: Plays base technique versus run. Drops to the hole versus pass.

WEAK END: Slants into and controls the C gap.

WEAK TANDEM: Plays base technique versus run. Covers the near back versus pass.

ROVER: Creeps toward the line of scrimmage during cadence and rushes from the edge. Contains the quarterback and weakside run. Chases strongside run.

FREE SAFETY: Cover the tight end. Disguise your assignment as Cover 1.

STRONG CORNER: Covers the flanker (inside technique).

WEAK CORNER: Covers the split end (inside technique).

STUNT DESCRIPTION: This is a *dog* that plugs up the middle and provides pressure from the edge. It also frees the Tandems and Mike to assist in run pursuit.

SECONDARY COVERAGE: Zero coverage disguised as cover 1. Tandems cover the running backs.

STUD: Creeps toward the line of scrimmage during cadence and rushes from the edge. Contains the quarterback and strongside run. Chases weakside run.

STRONG END: Attacks the near shoulder of the offensive guard and controls the B gap.

STRONG TANDEM: Plays base technique versus run. Covers the near back versus pass.

NOSE: Plays 0 technique.

MIKE: Plays base technique versus run. Drops to the hole versus pass.

WEAK END: Attacks the near shoulder of the offensive guard and controls the B gap.

WEAK TANDEM: Plays base technique versus run. Covers the near back versus pass.

ROVER: Creeps toward the line of scrimmage during cadence and rushes from the edge. Contains the quarterback and weakside run. Chases strongside run.

FREE SAFETY: Covers the tight end. Disguises his assignment as cover 1.

STRONG CORNER: Covers the flanker (inside technique).

WEAK CORNER: Covers the split end (inside technique).

STUNT #21

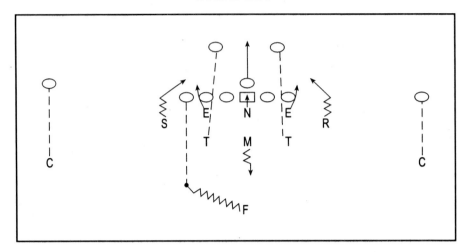

STUNT DESCRIPTION: This is a *dog* that is good against the option. The ends and Tandems will employ a tango read, which will be explained in detail in Chapter 8.

SECONDARY COVERAGE: Zero coverage disguised as cover 1. Tandems cover the running backs.

STUD: Creeps toward the line of scrimmage during cadence and rushes from the edge. Contains the quarterback and strongside run. Chases weakside run.

STRONG END: Slants into the C gap and employs a tango read with the strong Tandem.

STRONG TANDEM: Employs a Tango read with the strong end. Covers the near back versus pass.

NOSE: Plays 0 technique.

MIKE: Plays base technique versus run. Drops to the hole versus pass.

WEAK END: Slants into the C gap and employs a tango read with the weak Tandem.

WEAK TANDEM: Employs a Tango read with the weak end. Covers the near back versus pass.

ROVER: Creeps toward the line of scrimmage during cadence and rushes from the edge. Contains the quarterback and weakside run. Chases strongside run.

FREE SAFETY: Covers the tight end. Disguises his assignment as cover 1.

STRONG CORNER: Covers the flanker (inside technique).

WEAK CORNER: Covers the split end (inside technique).

STUNT #22

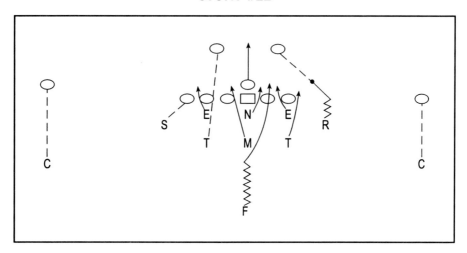

STUNT DESCRIPTION: This is an *illusion blitz* that provides the defense with a free safety blitz and a *weakside overload*. This is a good stunt in a passing situation but is vulnerable to strongside run.

SECONDARY COVERAGE: A variation of zero coverage. The strong Tandem and Rover cover the running backs

STUD: Covers the tight end. He can not be fooled by a delayed release; he has no help over the top.

STRONG END: Slants into and controls the C gap. Contains the quarterback versus pass.

STRONG TANDEM: Plays base technique versus run. Covers the near back versus pass.

NOSE: Slants into and controls the weakside A gap.

MIKE: Blitzes through the strongside A gap.

WEAK END: Quickly penetrates the B gap. Quick penetration of this gap is imperative!

WEAK TANDEM: Blitzes through the outside shoulder of the offensive tackle. Secures the C gap versus run and contains the quarterback versus pass.

ROVER: Creeps toward the line of scrimmage during cadence and gives the impression he intends to rush from the edge. Contains weakside run and chases strongside run. Spies the near back versus pass.

FREE SAFETY: Creeps toward the line of scrimmage during cadence and blitzes through the weak-side B gap.

STRONG CORNER: Covers the flanker (inside technique).

WEAK CORNER: Covers the split end (inside technique).

STUNT #23

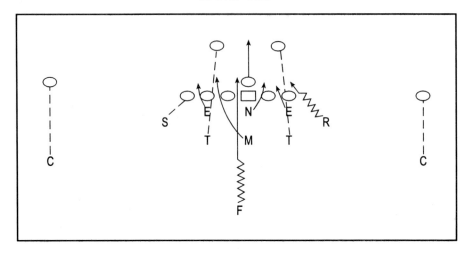

STUNT DESCRIPTION: This is a *blitz* that provides the defense with a free safety blitz and frees the Tandems to render good run pursuit.

SECONDARY COVERAGE: A variation of zero coverage. Tandems cover the running backs.

STUD: Covers the tight end. Can not be fooled by a delayed release; he has no help over the top.

STRONG END: Slants into and controls the C gap. Contains the quarterback versus pass.

STRONG TANDEM: Plays base technique versus run. Covers the near back versus pass.

NOSE: Slants into and controls the weakside A gap.

MIKE: Blitzes through the strongside B gap.

WEAK END: Attacks the near shoulder of the offensive guard and controls the B gap.

WEAK TANDEM: Scrapes outside and contains weakside run. Pursues strongside run from an inside-out position and covers the near back versus pass.

ROVER: Creeps toward the line of scrimmage during cadence and attacks the near shoulder of the offensive tackle. Secures the C gap versus run and contains the quarterback versus pass.

FREE SAFETY: Creeps toward the line of scrimmage during cadence and blitzes through the strongside A gap.

STRONG CORNER: Covers the flanker (inside technique).

WEAK CORNER: Covers the split end (inside technique).

STUNT #24

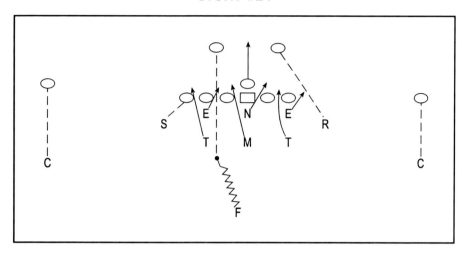

STUNT DESCRIPTION: This is a *blitz* that provides the defense with the threat of a free safety blitz.

SECONDARY COVERAGE: A variation of zero coverage. The Rover and the free safety cover the running backs.

STUD: Covers the tight end. Can not be fooled by a delayed release; he has no help over the top.

STRONG END: Slants into and controls the B gap.

STRONG TANDEM: Blitzes through and controls the strongside C gap. Contains the quarterback versus pass.

NOSE: Slants into and controls the weakside A gap.

MIKE: Blitzes through the strongside A gap.

WEAK END: Slants outside. Secures the C gap versus run and contains the quarterback versus pass.

WEAK TANDEM: Blitzes through and controls the B gap.

ROVER: Plays 8 technique versus run. Covers the near back versus pass.

FREE SAFETY: Creeps toward the line of scrimmage during cadence giving the impression that a strong safety blitz is in progress. Scrapes outside and contains strongside runs. Pursues weakside run from an inside-out position and covers the near back versus pass.

STRONG CORNER: Covers the flanker (inside technique).

WEAK CORNER: Covers the split end (inside technique).

STUNT #25

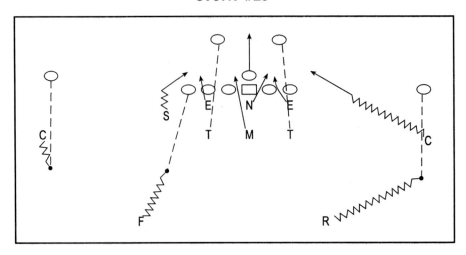

STUNT DESCRIPTION: This *blitz* provides the defense with a *weak cornerback* blitz and excellent pressure from the edge. The Tandems are also freed up to provide excellent run pursuit.

SECONDARY COVERAGE: Zero coverage disguised as cover 2. The Tandems play base technique versus run and cover the running backs versus pass.

STUD: Creeps toward the line of scrimmage during cadence and rushes from the edge. Contains the quarterback and strongside run. Chases weakside run.

STRONG END: Slants into and controls the C gap.

STRONG TANDEM: Plays base technique versus run and covers the near back versus pass.

NOSE: Slants into and controls the weakside A gap.

MIKE: Blitzes through the strongside A gap.

WEAK END: Attacks the near shoulder of the offensive guard and controls the B gap.

WEAK TANDEM: Plays base technique versus run. Covers the near back versus pass.

ROVER: Disguises his assignment as cover 2 but moves to a position that will enable him to cover X when the ball is snapped.

FREE SAFETY: Covers the tight end. Disguises his assignment as cover 2.

STRONG CORNER: Covers the flanker Z (inside technique). Disguises his assignment as cover 2.

WEAK CORNER: Creeps inside during cadence and rushes from the edge. Contains the quarterback and weakside run. Chases strongside run.

STUNT #26

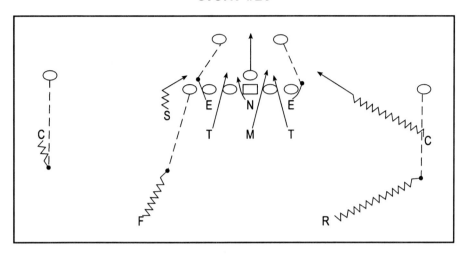

STUNT DESCRIPTION: This is an *illusion blitz* that provides the defense with a weak cornerback blitz.

SECONDARY COVERAGE: Zero coverage disguised as cover 2. The ends slant into the C gaps and spy the running backs versus pass.

STUD: Creeps toward the line of scrimmage during cadence and rushes from the edge. Contains the quarterback and strongside run. Chases weakside run.

STRONG END: Slants into the C gap and secures this gap versus run. Spies the near back versus pass.

STRONG TANDEM: Blitzes through and controls the B gap.

NOSE: Slants into and controls the strongside A gap.

MIKE: Blitzes through the weakside A gap.

WEAK END: Slants into the C gap and secures this gap versus run. Spies the near back versus pass.

WEAK TANDEM: Blitzes through and controls the B gap.

ROVER: Disguises his assignment as cover 2 but moves to a position that will enable him to cover X when the ball is snapped.

FREE SAFETY: Covers the tight end. Disguises his assignment as cover 2.

STRONG CORNER: Covers the flanker (inside technique). Disguises his assignment as cover 2.

WEAK CORNER: Creeps inside during cadence and rushes from the edge. Contains the quarterback and weakside run. Chases strongside run.

4

Cover 1 Stunts

Cover 1 is a man-to-man coverage with the free safety free. The strength of this coverage is that the free safety is keying the ball, playing center field, and backing up the two cornerbacks and the eight defenders in the box. Another strength of this coverage is that it is a man-to-man coverage and the offense can not high-low zones or attack seams. An additional strength with this coverage is that the cornerbacks can use bump, trail, or loose-man and easily disguise which technique they are using. This not only inhibits the quarterback's pre-snap read, but when the bump technique is employed, it disrupts the timing of the receivers' routes.

Despite the advantages of playing cover 1, cover 1 stunts do not exert as much pressure on the offense as zero coverage stunts. This weakness can be somewhat offset by incorporating *illusion dogs*, *fire zone blitzes*, and *hybrid fire zone blitzes* into the stunt package.

Whom Can the Free Safety Help?

Although cover 1 employs a free safety, the two cornerbacks can't realistically count on the free safety to assist them with all deep patterns. The field is simply too wide to expect the free safety to cover the entire area between the two sidelines. When a cornerback can expect inside help from the free safety, he should employ an outside-leverage technique. When a cornerback can't expect inside help, he should employ an inside leverage technique. Figures 4-1a through 4-1c show three common formation strength/field position situations that will determine the cornerback's leverage technique.

In Figure 4-1a, the strong cornerback cannot expect to receive inside help. He should therefore maintain inside leverage on the flanker. Although the weak cornerback could receive help from the free safety, he should employ an inside leverage technique and take away the split end's inside routes because the split end is close to the sideline and it is doubtful that he will attempt to run outside routes.

Because both receivers in Figure 4-1b have assumed tight splits, both cornerbacks can expect to receive inside help and should maintain outside leverage. Although the ball is in the middle of the field in Figure 4-1c, both the flanker and split end have assumed wide splits. The two cornerbacks should therefore maintain inside leverage because it is doubtful that the safety can help either of them with inside routes.

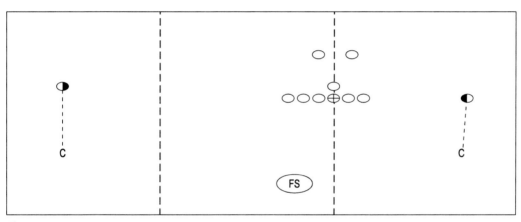

Figure 4-1a

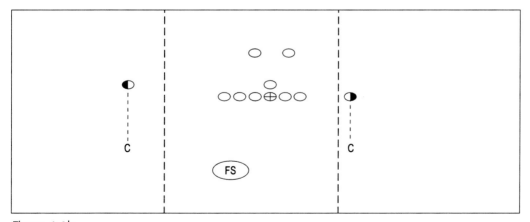

Figure 4-1b

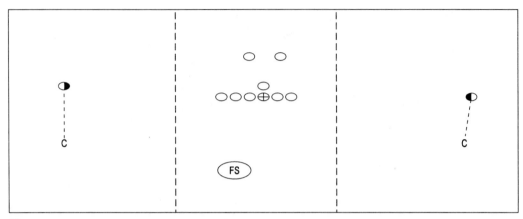

Figure 4-1c

Techniques and Assignments for
Fire Zone Blitz Drops

The fire zone blitz has become an extremely popular stunt tactic in recent years. As noted in Chapter One, when a fire zone blitz is employed, three defenders drop into the under coverage and share the joint responsibility of combo-covering the tight end and the two running backs. We refer to the under coverage drops as **Abel**, **Baker**, and **Charlie**. The techniques and assignments for these drops are as follows:

Assignments and Techniques for Abel's Drop:

- **Abel** drops to a position that will enable him to attain outside leverage on #2.

- Keys #2 to #3.

- If #2 runs a quick out (six yards or less), the defender immediately jumps his pattern and establishes a 3-yard cushion (Figure 4-2).

- If #2 runs a vertical route and #3 runs an out pattern of six yards or less, the defender gains depth and squeezes #2 inside. He should not be in a big hurry to jump #3's out pattern because #2 may turn his vertical route into a deep out. The defender relinquishes his cushion on #2 and tries to work to a depth of 8 to10 yards. As #3 starts to cross **Abel's** face, the defender begins to widen and establishes a loose cushion on #3, but tries to stay in the throwing lane between the quarterback and #2 for as long as possible. **Baker** will help by alerting **Abel** with an "out-out" call in the event that #2 does turn his vertical route into a deep out (Figure 4-3).

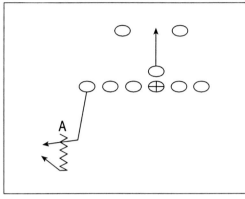

Figure 4-2

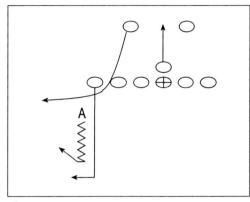

Figure 4-3

- If #2 runs a vertical route and #3 either blocks or runs a short inside route, **Abel** locks on to #2, squeezes him inside, maintains outside leverage, and forces him to run a collision course (Figure 4-4).

- If #2 runs a quick crossing pattern, the defender keys #3 to #4 (Figure 4-5).

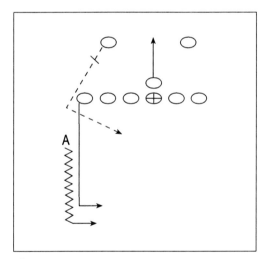

Figure 4-4

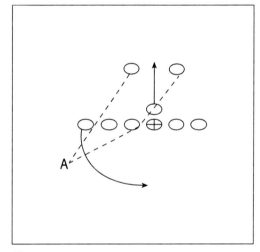

Figure 4-5

Assignments and Techniques for Baker's Drop:

- **Baker** drops to a position that enables him to establish inside leverage on #2, but keeps #3 in his periphery.

- Keys #2 to #3.

- If #2 runs a vertical route, **Baker** gains depth and covers him from an inside-out position, keeping #3 in his periphery. If #3 blocks or runs a short out pattern, the defender locks on to #2 (Figure 4-6a). If #3 runs a short in pattern, Baker releases his coverage of #2 and locks on to #3 (Figure 4-6b).

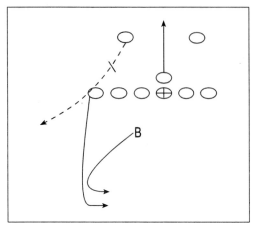 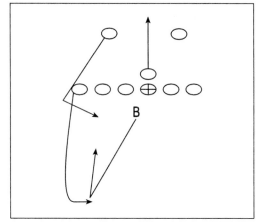

Figure 4-6a   Figure 4-6b

- If #2 runs a quick crossing pattern (six yards or less), **Baker** immediately calls "in-in", jams #2, walls him off, and forces him to deepen his pattern. The defender then locks on to #2 (Figure 4-7a) unless **Charlie** echoes **Baker's** "in-in""call. If **Charlie** echoes **Baker's** call, it is because #2 & #4 are crossing. If #2 and #4 cross, **Baker** releases his coverage of #2, gains depth, and locks on to #4 (Figure4-7b).

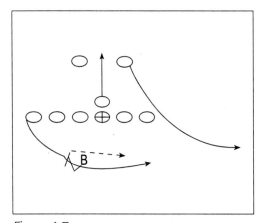 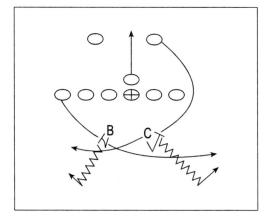

Figure 4-7a   Figure 4-7b

- If #2 runs a quick out pattern, **Baker** immediately redirects his attention to #3 and covers him (Figure 4-8a). If #3 and #4 try to run short crossing patterns, **Baker** follows the same rules as when #2 and #4 ran short crossing patterns (Figure 4-8b).

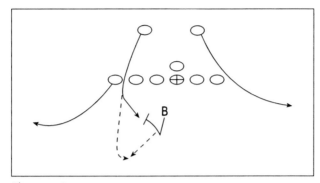

Figure 4-8a

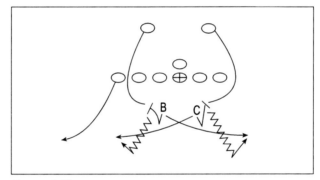

Figure 4-8b

Assignments and Techniques for Charlie's Drop:

- **Charlie** opens up and drops to a position that enables him to cover #4 from an inside-out position.

- Keys #4, but stays alert for an "in-in" call from **Baker**.

- If #4 runs a quick crossing pattern (six yards or less), **Charlie** immediately jams #4, walls him off, and forces him to deepen his pattern. **Charlie** locks on to #4 (Figure 4-9a) unless Baker has given you an "in-in" call (**Baker** will be the first one to give the call because #2 is aligned on the line of scrimmage and #4 is in the backfield). If **Baker** calls "in-in", **Charlie** echoes his call, releases his coverage of #4, gains depth, and locks on to #2 or #3 (Figure 4-9b).

- **Charlie** covers #4 on all other routes.

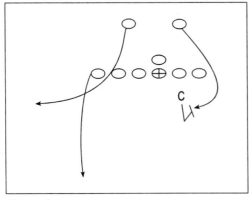

Figure 4-9a

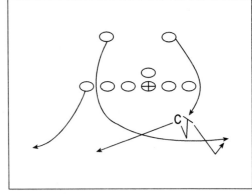

Figure 4-9b

Fire Zone Coverage Versus the Dirty Dozen

Figures 4-10a through 4-10l shows how the fire zone would adjust to and cover 12 of the toughest patterns it will ever face.

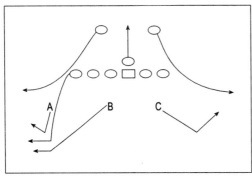

Figure 4-10a

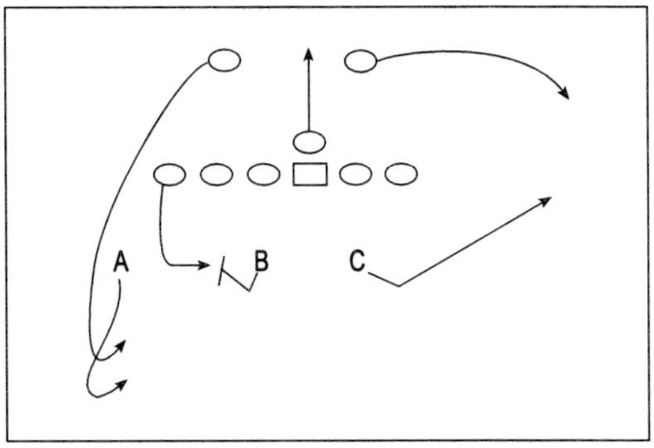

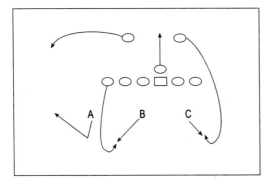

Figure 4-10b

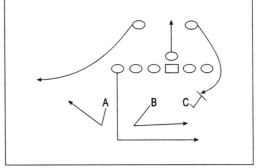

Figure 4-10c

Figure 4-10d

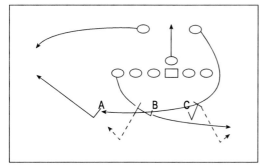

Figure 4-10e

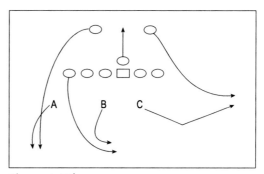

Figure 4-10f

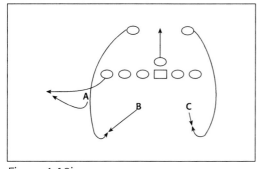

Figure 4-10g

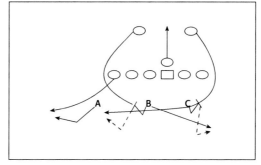

Figure 4-10h

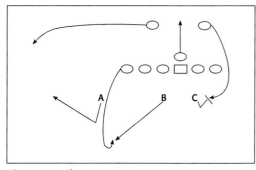

Figure 4-10i

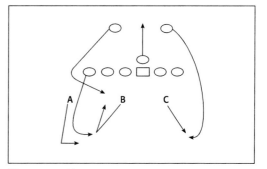

Figure 4-10j

Figure 4-10k

Figure 4-10l

Hybrid Fire Zone Coverage

Hybrid fire zone coverage is very similar to fire zone coverage. There are two main differences between the two. First, hybrid fire zone coverage assigns only two defenders to drop into the under coverage. These two players drop **Abel/Baker** and combo-cover the tight end and strongside halfback. Secondly, an illusion stunt will be employed on the weakside and one of the defenders involved in that stunt will be assigned to "spy" the weakside halfback.

Adjusting Cover 1 to Offensive Formations

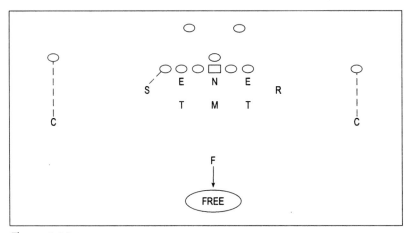

Figure 4-11a

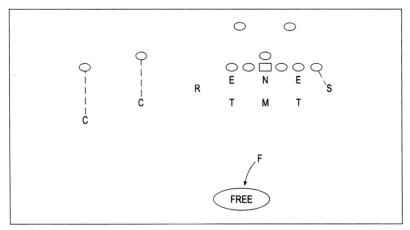

Figure 4-11b

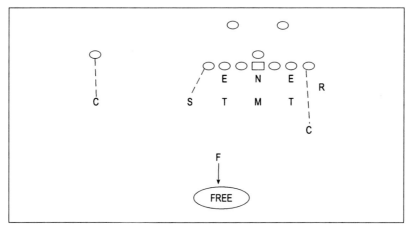

Figure 4-11c

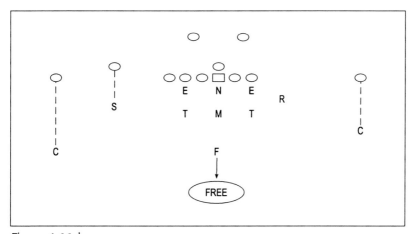

Figure 4-11d

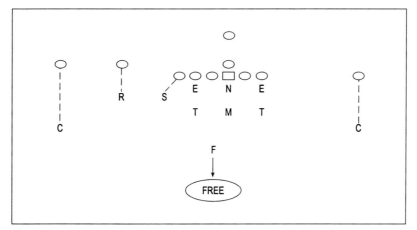

Figure 4-11e

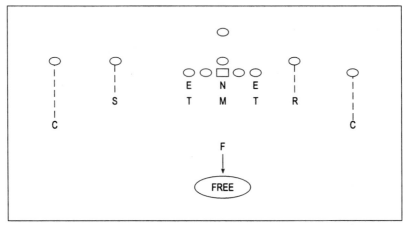

Figure 4-11f

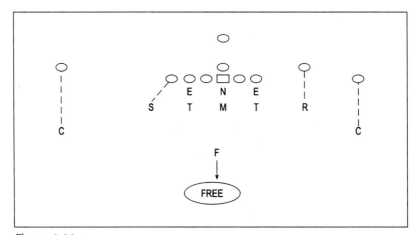

Figure 4-11g

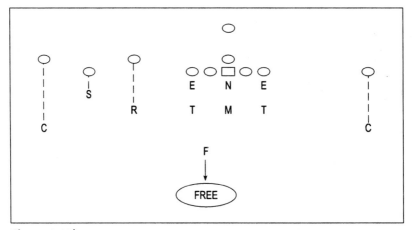

Figure 4-11h

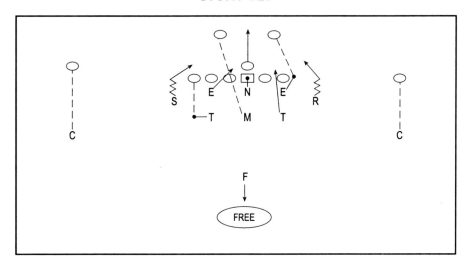

STUNT DESCRIPTION: This is a *dog* that gives the defense excellent pressure at the edge.

SECONDARY COVERAGE: Cover 1. The strong Tandem covers the tight end, Mike and the weak end cover the running backs, and the free safety is free.

STUD: Creeps toward the line of scrimmage during cadence and rushes from the edge. Contains the quarterback and strongside run. Chases weakside run.

STRONG END: Attacks the near shoulder of the offensive guard and controls the B gap.

STRONG TANDEM: Shuffles laterally at the snap and covers the tight end.

NOSE: Plays 0 technique.

MIKE: Plays base technique versus run. Covers the strong back versus pass.

WEAK END: Slants outside and secures the C gap versus run. Spies the near back versus pass.

WEAK TANDEM: Blitzes through and controls the B gap.

ROVER: Creeps toward the line of scrimmage during cadence and rushes from the edge. Contains the quarterback and weakside run. Chases strongside run.

FREE SAFETY: Lines up as though he's playing cover 3. Provides alley support to run. Plays centerfield versus pass.

STRONG CORNER: Covers #1. Inside/outside technique dependent upon field position and the distance of flanker's split.

WEAK CORNER: Covers #1. Inside/outside technique dependent upon field position and the distance of split end's split.

STUNT #28

STUNT DESCRIPTION: This is a *dog*.

SECONDARY COVERAGE: Cover 1. The Stud covers the tight end. The Tandems cover the running backs, and the free safety is free.

STUD: Plays 8 technique versus run. Covers the tight end versus pass.

STRONG END: Slants into and secures the C gap versus run. Contains the quarterback versus pass.

STRONG TANDEM: Plays base technique versus run. Covers the near back versus pass.

NOSE: Slants into and controls the weakside A gap.

MIKE: Blitzes through the strongside A gap.

WEAK END: Slants into the C gap and secures this gap versus run. Contains the quarterback versus pass.

WEAK TANDEM: Plays base technique versus run. Covers the near back versus pass.

ROVER: Creeps toward the line of scrimmage during cadence and rushes from the edge. Contains the quarterback and weakside run. Chases strongside run

FREE SAFETY: Lines up as though he's playing cover 3. Provides alley support to run. Plays centerfield versus pass.

STRONG CORNER: Covers #1. Inside/outside technique dependent upon field position and the distance of flanker's split.

WEAK CORNER: Covers #1. Inside/outside technique dependent upon field position and the distance of split end's split.

STUNT #29

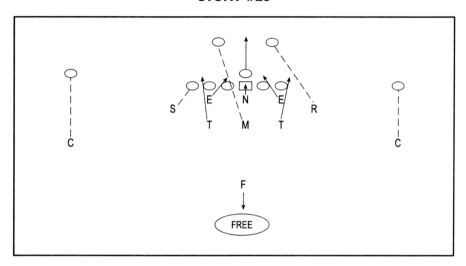

STUNT DESCRIPTION: This is a *dog*.

SECONDARY COVERAGE: Cover 1. The Stud covers the tight end, Mike and Rover cover the running backs, and the free safety is free.

STUD: Plays 8 technique versus run. Covers the tight end versus pass.

STRONG END: Attacks the near shoulder of the offensive guard and controls the B gap.

STRONG TANDEM: Stunts through the outside shoulder of the offensive tackle. Secures the C gap versus run and contains the quarterback versus pass.

NOSE: Plays 0 technique.

MIKE: Plays base technique versus run. Covers the strong back versus pass.

WEAK END: Attacks the near shoulder of the offensive guard and controls the B gap.

WEAK TANDEM: Stunts through the outside shoulder of the offensive tackle. Secures the C gap versus run and contains the quarterback versus pass.

ROVER: Plays 8 technique versus run. Covers the near back versus pass.

FREE SAFETY: Lines up as though he's playing cover 3. Provides alley support to run. Plays centerfield versus pass.

STRONG CORNER: Covers #1. Inside/outside technique dependent upon field position and the distance of flanker's split.

WEAK CORNER: Covers #1. Inside/outside technique dependent upon field position and the distance of split end's split.

STUNT #30

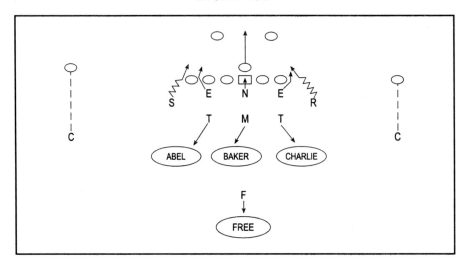

STUNT DESCRIPTION: This is a *fire zone blitz* that provides the defense with excellent pressure on the edge.

SECONDARY COVERAGE: Cover 1. The Tandems and Mike drop into coverage and the free safety is free.

STUD: Creeps toward the line of scrimmage during cadence and rushes from the edge. Contains the quarterback and strongside run. Chases weakside run.

STRONG END: Slants into and controls the C gap.

STRONG TANDEM: Plays base technique versus run. Drops **Abel** versus pass.

NOSE: Plays 0 technique.

MIKE: Plays base technique versus run. Drops **Baker** versus pass.

WEAK END: Slants into and controls the C gap.

WEAK TANDEM: Plays base technique versus run. Drops **Charlie** versus pass.

ROVER: Creeps toward the line of scrimmage during cadence and rushes from the edge. Contains the quarterback and weakside run. Chases strongside run.

FREE SAFETY: Line up as though he's playing cover 3. Provides alley support to run. Plays centerfield versus pass.

STRONG CORNER: Covers #1. Inside/outside technique dependent upon field position and the distance of flanker's split.

WEAK CORNER: Covers #1. Inside/outside technique dependent upon field position and the distance of split end's split.

STUNT #31

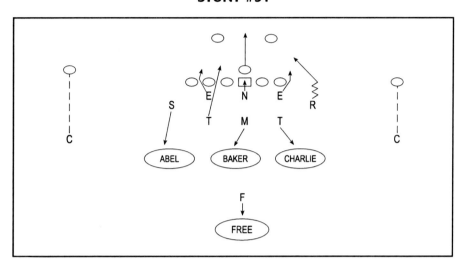

STUNT DESCRIPTION: This is a *fire zone blitz*.

SECONDARY COVERAGE: Cover 1. The weak Tandem, Mike, and Stud drop into coverage and the free safety is free.

STUD: Plays 8 technique versus run. Drops **Abel** versus pass.

STRONG END: Slants into and secures the C gap versus run. Contains the quarterback versus pass.

STRONG TANDEM: Blitzes through and controls the B gap.

NOSE: Plays 0 technique.

MIKE: Plays base technique versus run. Drops **Baker** versus pass.

WEAK END: Slants into and controls the C gap.

WEAK TANDEM: Plays base technique versus run. Drops **Charlie** versus pass.

ROVER: Creeps toward the line of scrimmage during cadence and rushes from the edge. Contains the quarterback and weakside run. Chases strongside run.

FREE SAFETY: Lines up as though he's playing cover 3. Provides alley support to run. Plays centerfield versus pass.

STRONG CORNER: Covers #1. Inside/outside technique dependent upon field position and the distance of flanker's split.

WEAK CORNER: Covers #1. Inside/outside technique dependent upon field position and the distance of split end's split.

STUNT #32

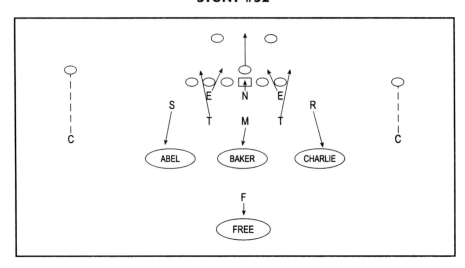

STUNT DESCRIPTION: This is a *fire zone blitz*.

SECONDARY COVERAGE: Cover 1. The Mike, Rover, and Stud drop into coverage and the free safety is free.

STUD: Plays 8 technique versus run. Drops **Abel** versus pass.

STRONG END: Attacks the near shoulder of the offensive guard and controls the B gap.

STRONG TANDEM: Blitzes through and secures the C gap versus run and contains the quarterback versus pass.

NOSE: Plays 0 technique.

MIKE: Plays base technique versus run. Drops **Baker** versus pass.

WEAK END: Attacks the near shoulder of the offensive guard and controls the B gap.

WEAK TANDEM: Blitzes through and secures the C gap versus run and contains the quarterback versus pass.

ROVER: Plays 8 technique versus run. Drops **Charlie** versus pass.

FREE SAFETY: Lines up as though he's playing cover 3. Provides alley support to run. Plays centerfield versus pass.

STRONG CORNER: Covers #1. Inside/outside technique dependent upon field position and the distance of flanker's split.

WEAK CORNER: Covers #1. Inside/outside technique dependent upon field position and the distance of split end's split.

STUNT #33

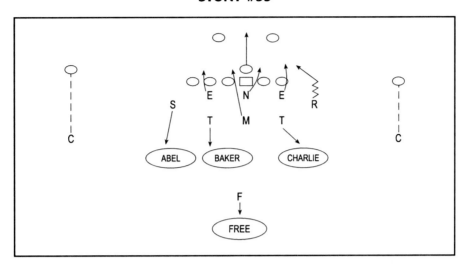

STUNT DESCRIPTION: This is a *fire zone blitz*.

SECONDARY COVERAGE: Cover 1. The Tandems and Stud drop into coverage and the free safety is free.

STUD: Plays 8 technique versus run. Drops **Abel** versus pass.

STRONG END: Slants into and controls the C gap. Contains the quarterback versus pass.

STRONG TANDEM: Plays base technique versus run. Drops **Baker** versus pass.

NOSE: Slants into and controls the weakside A gap.

MIKE: Blitzes through the strongside A gap.

WEAK END: Slants into and controls the C gap.

WEAK TANDEM: Plays base technique versus run. Drops **Charlie** versus pass.

ROVER: Creeps toward the line of scrimmage during cadence and rushes from the edge. Contains the quarterback and weakside run. Chases strongside run.

FREE SAFETY: Lines up as though he's playing cover 3. Provides alley support to run. Plays centerfield versus pass.

STRONG CORNER: Covers #1. Inside/outside technique dependent upon field position and the distance of flanker's split.

WEAK CORNER: Covers #1. Inside/outside technique dependent upon field position and the distance of split end's split.

STUNT #34

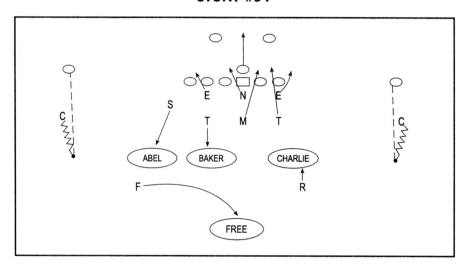

STUNT DESCRIPTION: This is a *fire zone blitz*.

SECONDARY COVERAGE: Cover 1 disguised as cover 2. The strong Tandem, Rover and Stud drop into coverage and the free safety is free.

STUD: Plays 8 technique versus run. Drops **Abel** versus pass.

STRONG END: Slants into and controls the C gap versus run. Contains the quarterback versus pass.

STRONG TANDEM: Plays base technique versus run. Drops **Baker** versus pass.

NOSE: Slants into and controls the strongside A gap.

MIKE: Blitzes through the weakside A gap.

WEAK END: Slants into and controls the C gap versus run. Contains the quarterback versus pass.

WEAK TANDEM: Blitzes through and controls the B gap.

ROVER: Lines up as though he's playing cover 2. Employs an 8 technique versus run and drops Charlie versus pass.

FREE SAFETY: Lines up as though he's playing cover 2. Provides alley support to run. Plays centerfield versus pass.

STRONG CORNER: Lines up as though he's playing cover 2. Covers the flanker. Inside/outside technique dependent upon field position and the distance of flanker's split.

WEAK CORNER: Lines up as though he's playing cover 2. Covers the split end. Inside/outside technique dependent upon field position and the distance of split end's split.

STUNT #35

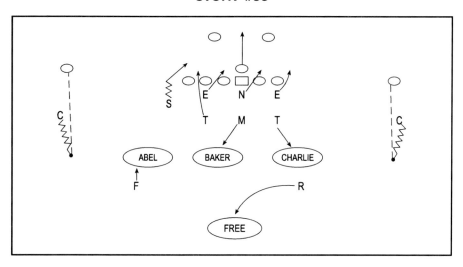

STUNT DESCRIPTION: This is a *fire zone blitz* that provides the defense with a weakside line slant.

SECONDARY COVERAGE: Cover 1 disguised as cover 2. The weak Tandem, Mike and free safety drop into coverage and the Rover is free.

STUD: Creeps toward the line of scrimmage during cadence and rushes from the edge. Contains the quarterback and strongside run. Chases weakside run.

STRONG END: Attacks the near shoulder of the offensive guard and controls the B gap.

STRONG TANDEM: Blitzes through and controls the C gap.

NOSE: Slants into and controls the weakside A gap.

MIKE: Plays base technique versus run. Drops **Baker** versus pass.

WEAK END: Slants into and controls the C gap versus run. Contains the quarterback versus pass.

WEAK TANDEM: Plays base technique versus run. Drops **Charlie** versus pass.

ROVER: Lines up as though he's playing cover 2. Employs an 8 technique versus run. Plays centerfield versus pass.

FREE SAFETY: Lines up as though he's playing cover 2. Provides alley support to run and drops **Abel** versus pass.

STRONG CORNER: Lines up as though he's playing cover 2. Covers the flanker. Inside/outside technique dependent upon field position and the distance of flanker's split.

WEAK CORNER: Lines up as though he's playing cover 2. Covers the split end. Inside/outside technique dependent upon field position and the distance of split end's split.

STUNT #36

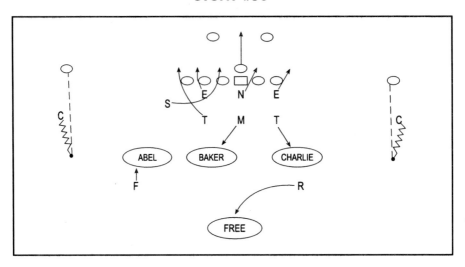

STUNT DESCRIPTION: This is a *fire zone blitz*.

SECONDARY COVERAGE: Cover 1 disguised as cover 2. The weak Tandem, Mike and free safety drop into coverage and the Rover is free.

STUD: Blitzes through the strongside B gap.

STRONG END: Slants into and controls the C gap.

STRONG TANDEM: Attacks the outside shoulder of the tight end. Contains the quarterback and strongside run. Chases weakside run.

NOSE: Slants into and controls the weakside A gap.

MIKE: Plays base technique versus run. Drops **Baker** versus pass.

WEAK END: Slants into and controls the C gap versus run. Contains the quarterback versus pass.

WEAK TANDEM: Plays base technique versus run. Drops **Charlie** versus pass.

ROVER: Lines up as though he's playing cover 2. Employs an 8 technique versus run. Plays centerfield versus pass.

FREE SAFETY: Lines up as though he's playing cover 2. Provides alley support to run and drops **Abel** versus pass.

STRONG CORNER: Lines up as though he's playing cover 2. Covers the flanker. Inside/outside technique dependent upon field position and the distance of flanker's split.

WEAK CORNER: Lines up as though he's playing cover 2. Covers the split end. Inside/outside technique dependent upon field position and the distance of split end's split.

STUNT #37

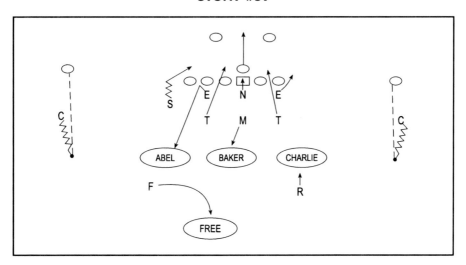

STUNT DESCRIPTION: This is a fire zone blitz that drops a defensive lineman into coverage.

SECONDARY COVERAGE: Cover 1 disguised as cover 2. The strong end, Rover and Mike drop into coverage and the free safety is free.

STUD: Creeps toward the line of scrimmage during cadence and rushes from the edge. Contains the quarterback and strongside run. Chases weakside run.

STRONG END: Slants into and controls the C gap. Drops **Abel** versus pass.

STRONG TANDEM: Blitzes through the outside shoulder of the offensive guard and controls the B gap.

NOSE: Plays 0 technique.

MIKE: Plays base technique versus run. Drops **Baker** versus pass.

WEAK END: Slants into and control the C gap. Contains the quarterback versus pass.

WEAK TANDEM: Blitzes through the outside shoulder of the offensive guard and controls the B gap.

ROVER: Lines up as though he's playing cover 2. Employs an 8 technique versus run and drops **Charlie** versus pass.

FREE SAFETY: Lines up as though he's playing cover 2. Provides alley support to run. Plays centerfield versus pass.

STRONG CORNER: Lines up as though he's playing cover 2. Covers the flanker. Inside/outside technique dependent upon field position and the distance of flanker's split.

WEAK CORNER: Lines up as though he's playing cover 2. Covers the split end Inside/outside technique dependent upon field position and the distance of split end's split.

STUNT #38

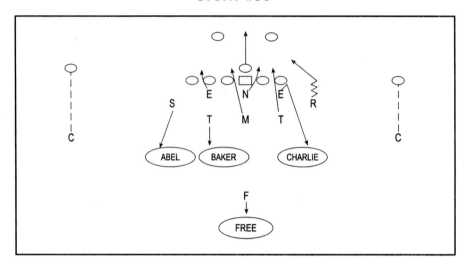

STUNT DESCRIPTION: This is a *fire zone blitz* that drops a defensive lineman into coverage.

SECONDARY COVERAGE: Cover 1. The strong Tandem, Stud, and weak end drop into coverage and the free safety is free.

STUD: Plays 8 technique versus run. Drops **Abel** versus pass.

STRONG END: Slants into and controls the C gap. Contains the quarterback versus pass.

STRONG TANDEM: Plays base technique versus run. Drops **Baker** versus pass.

NOSE: Slants into and controls the weakside A gap.

MIKE: Blitzes through the strongside A gap.

WEAK END: Slants into and controls the C gap. Drops **Charlie** versus pass.

WEAK TANDEM: Blitzes through and controls the B gap.

ROVER: Creeps toward the line of scrimmage during cadence and rushes from the edge. Contains the quarterback and weakside run. Chases strongside run.

FREE SAFETY: Lines up as though he's playing cover 3. Provides alley support to run. Plays centerfield versus pass.

STRONG CORNER: Covers #1. Inside/outside technique dependent upon field position and the distance of flanker's split.

WEAK CORNER: Covers #1. Inside/outside technique dependent upon field position and the distance of split end's split.

STUNT #39

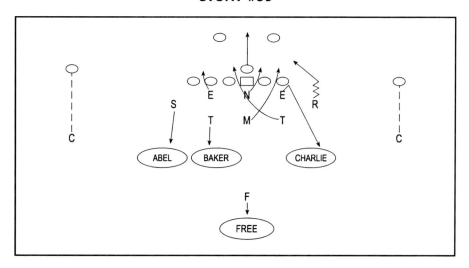

STUNT DESCRIPTION: This is a *fire zone blitz* that drops a defensive lineman into coverage.

SECONDARY COVERAGE: Cover 1. The strong Tandem, Stud, and weak end drop into coverage and the free safety is free.

STUD: Plays 8 technique versus run. Drop **Abel** versus pass.

STRONG END: Slants into and controls the C gap. Contains the quarterback versus pass.

STRONG TANDEM: Plays base technique versus run. Drops **Baker** versus pass.

NOSE: Slants into and controls the weakside A gap.

MIKE: Blitzes through the weakside B gap. He goes first.

WEAK END: Slants into and controls the C gap. Drops **Charlie** versus pass.

WEAK TANDEM: Blitzes through the strongside A gap. Mike goes first. He will therefore make his first step parallel to the line with his left foot.

ROVER: Creeps toward the line of scrimmage during cadence and rushes from the edge. Contains the quarterback and weakside run. Chases strongside run.

FREE SAFETY: Lines up as though he's playing cover 3. Provides alley support to run. Plays centerfield versus pass.

STRONG CORNER: Covers #1. Inside/outside technique dependent upon field position and the distance of flanker's split.

WEAK CORNER: Covers #1. Inside/outside technique dependent upon field position and the distance of split end's split.

STUNT #40

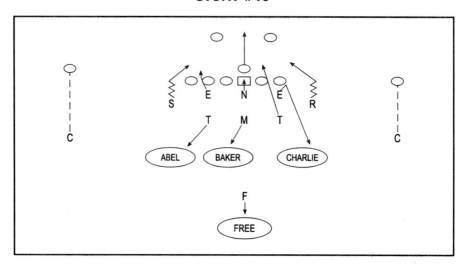

STUNT DESCRIPTION: This is a *fire zone blitz* that drops a defensive lineman into coverage and provides the defense with excellent pressure from the edge.

SECONDARY COVERAGE: Cover 1. The strong Tandem, Mike, and weak end drop into coverage and the free safety is free.

STUD: Creeps toward the line of scrimmage during cadence and rushes from the edge. Contains the quarterback and strongside run. Chases weakside run.

STRONG END: Slants into and controls the C gap.

STRONG TANDEM: Plays base technique versus run. Drops **Abel** versus pass.

NOSE: Plays 0 technique.

MIKE: Plays base technique versus run. Drops **Baker** versus pass.

WEAK END: Slants into and controls the C gap. Drops **Charlie** versus pass.

WEAK TANDEM: Blitzes through and controls the B gap.

ROVER: Creeps toward the line of scrimmage during cadence and rushes from the edge. Contains the quarterback and weakside run. Chases strongside run.

FREE SAFETY: Lines up as though he's playing cover 3. Provides alley support to run. Plays centerfield versus pass.

STRONG CORNER: Covers #1. Inside/outside technique dependent upon field position and the distance of flanker's split.

WEAK CORNER: Covers #1. Inside/outside technique dependent upon field position and the distance of split end's split.

STUNT #41

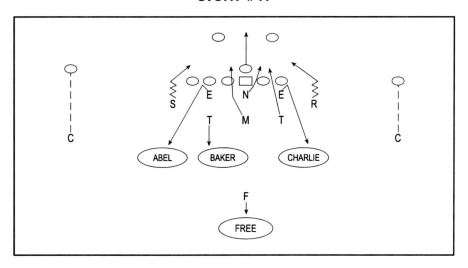

STUNT DESCRIPTION: This is *fire zone blitz* that drops two defensive linemen into coverage and provides the defense with excellent pressure from the edge.

SECONDARY COVERAGE: Cover 1. The strong Tandem, the strong end, and weak end drop into coverage and the free safety is free.

STUD: Creeps toward the line of scrimmage during cadence and rushes from the edge. Contains the quarterback and strongside run. Chases weakside run.

STRONG END: Slants into and secures C gap. Drops **Abel** versus pass.

STRONG TANDEM: Plays base technique versus run. Drops **Baker** versus pass.

NOSE: Slants into the weakside A gap.

MIKE: Blitzes through and controls the strongside A gap.

WEAK END: Slants into and secures the C gap. Drops **Charlie** versus pass.

WEAK TANDEM: Blitzes through and controls the B gap.

ROVER: Creeps toward the line of scrimmage during cadence and rushes from the edge. Contains the quarterback and weakside run. Chases strongside run.

FREE SAFETY: Lines up as though he's playing cover 3. Provides alley support to run. Plays centerfield versus pass.

STRONG CORNER: Covers #1. Inside/outside technique dependent upon field position and the distance of flanker's split.

WEAK CORNER: Covers #1. Inside/outside technique dependent upon field position and the distance of split end's split.

STUNT #42

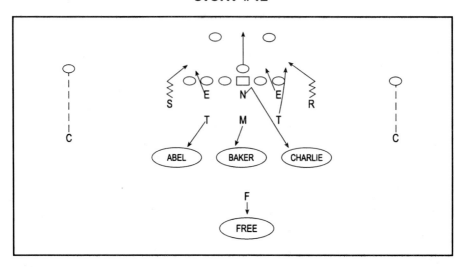

STUNT DESCRIPTION: This is *fire zone blitz* that drops a defensive linemen into coverage and provides the defense with excellent pressure from the edge.

SECONDARY COVERAGE: Cover 1. The strong Tandem, Mike, and Nose drop into coverage and the free safety is free.

STUD: Creeps toward the line of scrimmage during cadence and rushes from the edge. Contains the quarterback and strongside run. Chases weakside run.

STRONG END: Slants into and controls the C gap.

STRONG TANDEM: Plays base technique versus run. Drops **Abel** versus pass.

NOSE: Slants to and secures the weakside A gap versus run and drops **Charlie** versus pass.

MIKE: Plays base technique versus run. Drops **Baker** versus pass.

WEAK END: Attacks the near shoulder of the offensive guard and controls the B gap.

WEAK TANDEM: Blitzes through the outside shoulder of the offensive tackle and controls the C gap.

ROVER: Creeps toward the line of scrimmage during cadence and rushes from the edge. Contains the quarterback and weakside run. Chases strongside run.

FREE SAFETY: Lines up as though he's playing cover 3. Provides alley support to run. Plays centerfield versus pass.

STRONG CORNER: Covers #1. Inside/outside technique dependent upon field position and the distance of flanker's split.

WEAK CORNER: Covers #1. Inside/outside technique dependent upon field position and the distance of split end's split.

STUNT #43

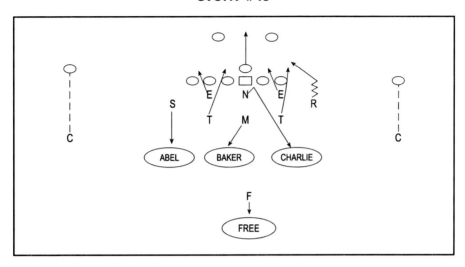

STUNT DESCRIPTION: This is fire zone blitz that drops a defensive linemen into coverage.

SECONDARY COVERAGE: Cover 1. The Stud, Mike, and Nose drop into coverage and the free safety is free.

STUD: Plays 8 technique versus run. Drops **Abel** versus pass.

STRONG END: Slants into and controls the C gap. Contains the quarterback versus pass.

STRONG TANDEM: Blitzes through the outside shoulder of the offensive guard and controls the B gap.

NOSE: Slants to and secures the weakside A gap versus run. Drops **Charlie** versus pass.

MIKE: Plays base technique versus run. Drops **Baker** versus pass.

WEAK END: Attacks the near shoulder of the offensive guard and controls the B gap.

WEAK TANDEM: Blitzes through the outside shoulder of the offensive tackle and controls the C gap.

ROVER: Creeps toward the line of scrimmage during cadence and rushes from the edge. Contains the quarterback and weakside run. Chases strongside run.

FREE SAFETY: Lines up as though he's playing cover 3. provides alley support to run. Plays centerfield versus pass.

STRONG CORNER: Covers #1. Inside/outside technique dependent upon field position and the distance of flanker's split.

WEAK CORNER: Covers #1. Inside/outside technique dependent upon field position and the distance of split end's split.

STUNT #44

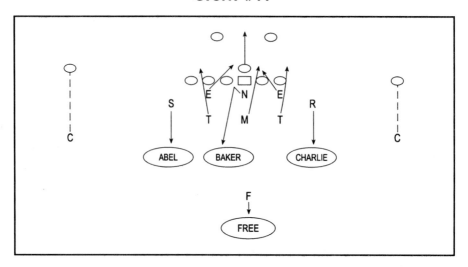

STUNT DESCRIPTION: This is *fire zone blitz* that sends both Tandems on a blitz and drops a defensive linemen into coverage.

SECONDARY COVERAGE: Cover 1. The Stud, Nose, and Rover drop into coverage and the free safety is free.

STUD: Plays 8 technique versus run. Drops **Abel** versus pass.

STRONG END: Attacks the near shoulder of the offensive guard and controls the B gap.

STRONG TANDEM: Blitzes through the outside shoulder of the offensive tackle and controls the C gap. Contains the quarterback versus pass.

NOSE: Slants to and secures the strongside A gap versus run. Drops **Baker** versus pass.

MIKE: Blitzes through the weakside A gap.

WEAK END: Attacks the near shoulder of the offensive guard and controls the B gap.

WEAK TANDEM: Blitzes through the outside shoulder of the offensive tackle and controls the C gap. Contains the quarterback versus pass.

ROVER: Plays 8 technique versus run. Drops **Charlie** versus pass.

FREE SAFETY: Lines up as though he's playing cover 3. Provides alley support to run. Plays centerfield versus pass.

STRONG CORNER: Covers #1. Inside/outside technique dependent upon field position and the distance of flanker's split.

WEAK CORNER: Covers #1. Inside/outside technique dependent upon field position and the distance of split end's split).

STUNT #45

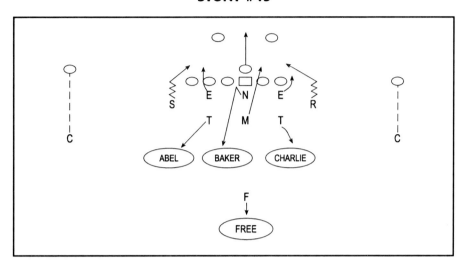

STUNT DESCRIPTION: This is a *fire zone blitz* that drops a defensive lineman into coverage and provides the defense with excellent pressure from the edge.

SECONDARY COVERAGE: Cover 1. The Tandems and the Nose drop into coverage and the free safety is free.

STUD: Creeps toward the line of scrimmage during cadence and rushes from the edge. Contains the quarterback and strongside run. Chases weakside run.

STRONG END: Slants into and controls the C gap.

STRONG TANDEM: Plays base technique versus run. Drops **Abel** versus pass.

NOSE: Slants to and secures the strongside A gap versus run. Drops **Baker** versus pass.

MIKE: Blitzes through the weakside A gap.

WEAK END: Slants to and controls the C gap.

WEAK TANDEM: Plays Base technique versus run. Drops **Charlie** versus pass.

ROVER: Creeps toward the line of scrimmage during cadence and rushes from the edge. Contains the quarterback and weakside run. Chases strongside run.

FREE SAFETY: Lines up as though he's playing cover 3. Provides alley support to run. Plays centerfield versus pass.

STRONG CORNER: Covers #1. Inside/outside technique dependent upon field position and the distance of flanker's split.

WEAK CORNER: Covers #1. Inside/outside technique dependent upon field position and the distance of split end's split.

STUNT #46

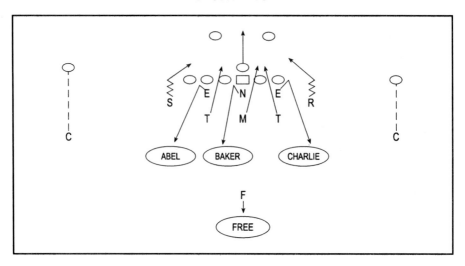

STUNT DESCRIPTION: This is a *fire zone blitz* that drops three defensive lineman into coverage and gives the offense the illusion that we're *sending the house*.

SECONDARY COVERAGE: Cover 1. The ends and the Nose drop into coverage and the free safety is free.

STUD: Creeps toward the line of scrimmage during cadence and rushes from the edge. Contains the quarterback and strongside run. Chases weakside run.

STRONG END: Slants to and secures the C gap versus run. Drops **Abel** versus pass.

STRONG TANDEM: Blitzes through the B gap.

NOSE: Slants to and secures the strongside A gap versus run. Drops **Baker** versus pass.

MIKE: Blitzes through the weakside A gap.

WEAK END: Slants to and controls the C gap. Drops **Charlie** versus pass.

WEAK TANDEM: Blitzes through the B gap.

ROVER: Creeps toward the line of scrimmage during cadence and rushes from the edge. Contains the quarterback and weakside run. Chases strongside run.

FREE SAFETY: Lines up as though he's playing cover 3. Provides alley support to run. Plays centerfield versus pass.

STRONG CORNER: Covers #1. Inside/outside technique dependent upon field position and the distance of flanker's split.

WEAK CORNER: Covers #1. Inside/outside technique dependent upon field position and the distance of split end's split.

STUNT #47

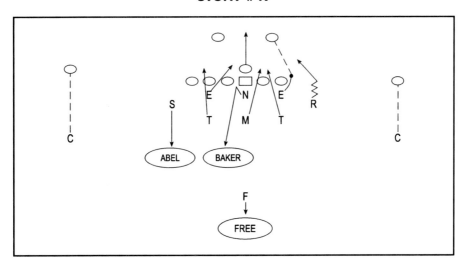

STUNT DESCRIPTION: This is a *hybrid fire zone blitz* that drops a defensive lineman into coverage.

SECONDARY COVERAGE: Cover 1. The Stud and Nose drop into coverage, the weak end spies the weak back, and the free safety is free.

STUD: Plays 8 technique versus run. Drops **Abel** versus

STRONG END: Attacks the near shoulder of the offensive guard and controls the B gap.

STRONG TANDEM: Blitzes through the outside shoulder of the offensive tackle and secures the C gap versus the run. Contains the quarterback versus pass.

NOSE: Slants to and secures the strong side A gap versus run. Drops **Baker** versus pass.

MIKE: Blitzes through the weakside A gap.

WEAK END: Slants into and controls the C gap. Spies the near back versus pass.

WEAK TANDEM: Blitzes through the B gap.

ROVER: Creeps toward the line of scrimmage during cadence and rushes from the edge. Contains the quarterback and weakside run. Chases strongside run.

FREE SAFETY: Lines up as though he's playing cover 3. Provides alley support to run. Plays centerfield versus pass.

STRONG CORNER: Covers #1. Inside/outside technique dependent upon field position and the distance of flanker's split.

WEAK CORNER: Covers #1. Inside/outside technique dependent upon field position and the distance of split end's split.

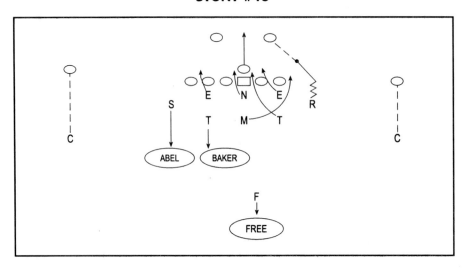

STUNT DESCRIPTION: This is a *hybrid fire zone blitz.*

SECONDARY COVERAGE: Cover 1. The Stud and the strong Tandem drop into coverage, the Rover spies the weak back, and the free safety is free.

STUD: Plays 8 technique versus run. Drops **Abel** versus

STRONG END: Slants into and controls the C gap. Contains the quarterback versus pass.

STRONG TANDEM: Plays base technique versus run. Drops **Baker** versus pass.

NOSE: Slants into and controls the strongside A gap.

MIKE: Blitzes through the outside shoulder of the offensive tackle and controls the weakside C gap. Contains the quarterback versus pass.

WEAK END: Slants into and controls the B gap.

WEAK TANDEM: Blitzes through the A gap.

ROVER: Creeps toward the line of scrimmage during cadence and rushes from the edge. Contains weakside run and chases strongside run. Spies the near back versus pass.

FREE SAFETY: Lines up as though he's playing cover 3. Provides alley support to run. Plays centerfield versus pass.

STRONG CORNER: Covers #1. Inside/outside technique dependent upon field position and the distance of flanker's split.

WEAK CORNER: Covers #1. Inside/outside technique dependent upon field position and the distance of split end's split.

STUNT #49

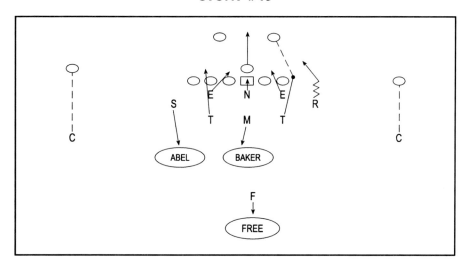

STUNT DESCRIPTION: This is a *hybrid fire zone blitz*.

SECONDARY COVERAGE: Cover 1. The Stud and Mike drop into coverage, the weak Tandem spies the weak back, and the free safety is free.

STUD: Plays 8 technique versus run. Drops **Abel** versus

STRONG END: Attacks the near shoulder of the offensive guard and controls the B gap.

STRONG TANDEM: Blitzes through the outside shoulder of the offensive tackle and controls the C gap. Contains the quarterback versus pass.

NOSE: Plays 0 technique.

MIKE: Plays base technique versus run. Drops **Baker** versus pass.

WEAK END: Attacks the near shoulder of the offensive guard and controls the B gap.

WEAK TANDEM: Blitzes through the outside shoulder of the offensive tackle and controls the C gap. Spies the near back versus pass.

ROVER: Creeps toward the line of scrimmage during cadence and rushes from the edge. Contains the quarterback and weakside run. Chases strongside run.

FREE SAFETY: Lines up as though he's playing cover 3. Provides alley support to run. Plays centerfield versus pass.

STRONG CORNER: Covers #1. Inside/outside technique dependent upon field position and the distance of flanker's split.

WEAK CORNER: Covers #1. Inside/outside technique dependent upon field position and the distance of split end's split.

STUNT #50

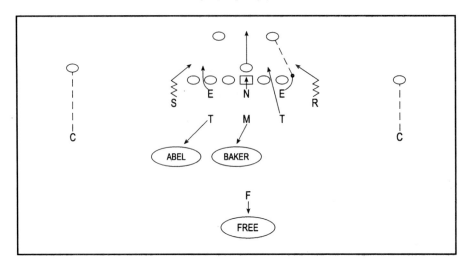

STUNT DESCRIPTION: This is a *hybrid fire zone blitz* that gives excellent pressure from the edge.

SECONDARY COVERAGE: Cover 1. The strong Tandem and Mike drop into coverage, the weak end spies the weak back, and the free safety is free.

STUD: Creeps toward the line of scrimmage during cadence and rushes from the edge. Contains strongside run and chases weakside run. Contains the quarterback versus pass.

STRONG END: Slants into and controls the C gap.

STRONG TANDEM: Plays base technique versus run. Drops **Abel** versus pass.

NOSE: Plays 0 technique.

MIKE: Plays base technique versus run. Drops **Baker** versus pass.

WEAK END: Slants into and controls the C gap. Spies the near back versus pass.

WEAK TANDEM: Blitzes through and controls the B gap.

ROVER: Creeps toward the line of scrimmage during cadence and rushes from the edge. Contains the quarterback and weakside run. Chases strongside run.

FREE SAFETY: Lines up as though he's playing cover 3. Provides alley support to run. Plays centerfield versus pass.

STRONG CORNER: Covers #1. Inside/outside technique dependent upon field position and the distance of flanker's split.

WEAK CORNER: Covers #1. Inside/outside technique dependent upon field position and the distance of split end's split.

STUNT #51

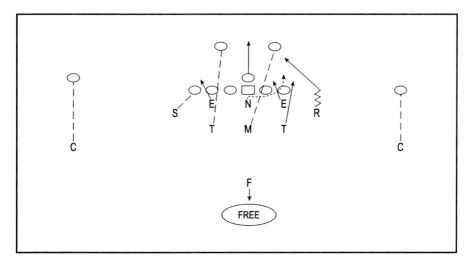

STUNT DESCRIPTION: This is a *dog* that creates a weakside overload via a *delayed line twist*.

SECONDARY COVERAGE: Cover 1. The Stud covers the tight end, the Mike and the strong Tandem cover the backs, and the free safety is free.

STUD: Plays 8 technique versus run. Covers the tight end versus pass.

STRONG END: Slants into and controls the C gap. Contains the quarterback versus pass.

STRONG TANDEM: Plays base technique versus run. Covers the near back versus pass.

NOSE: Plays 0 technique versus run. Loops into the weakside B gap versus pass.

MIKE: Plays base technique versus run. Covers the weak back versus pass.

WEAK END: Slants into and quickly penetrates the B gap. Penetration of this gap is imperative!

WEAK TANDEM: Blitzes through the outside shoulder of the offensive tackle and controls the C gap.

ROVER: Creeps toward the line of scrimmage during cadence and rushes from the edge. Contains the quarterback and weakside run. Chases strongside run.

FREE SAFETY: Lines up as though he's playing cover 3. Provides alley support to run. Plays centerfield versus pass.

STRONG CORNER: Covers #1. Inside/outside technique dependent upon field position and the distance of flanker's split.

WEAK CORNER: Covers #1. Inside/outside technique dependent upon field position and the distance of split end's split.

STUNT #52

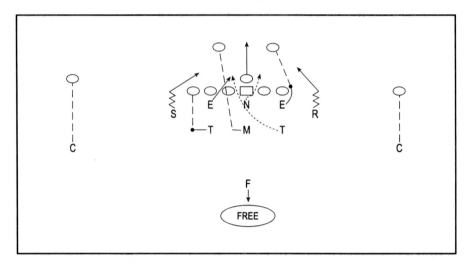

STUNT DESCRIPTION: This is a *dog* that provides the defense with excellent pressure from the edge and a *delayed linebacker blitz*.

SECONDARY COVERAGE: Cover 1. The strong Tandem covers the tight end, the Mike and the weak end cover the backs, and the free safety is free.

STUD: Creeps toward the line of scrimmage during cadence and rushes from the edge. Contains the quarterback and strongside run. Chases weakside run.

STRONG END: Slants through the outside shoulder of the offensive guard and controls the B gap.

STRONG TANDEM: Shuffles outside at the snap and covers the tight end.

NOSE: Plays 0 technique versus run. Quickly penetrates the weakside A gap versus pass.

MIKE: Plays base technique versus run. Covers the strong back versus pass.

WEAK END: Slants outside and controls the C gap. Spies the near back versus pass.

WEAK TANDEM: Plays base technique versus run. Delay blitzes through the strongside A gap versus pass.

ROVER: Creeps toward the line during cadence and rushes from the edge. Contains the quarterback and weakside run. Chases strongside run.

FREE SAFETY: Lines up as though he's playing cover 3. Provides alley support to run. Plays centerfield versus pass.

STRONG CORNER: Covers #1. Inside/outside technique dependent upon field position and the distance of flanker's split.

WEAK CORNER: Covers #1. Inside/outside technique dependent upon field position and the distance of split end's split.

STUNT #53

STUNT DESCRIPTION: This is a *dog* that provides the defense with a *delayed linebacker blitz*.

SECONDARY COVERAGE: Cover 1. The Stud covers the tight end, the Mike and strong Tandem cover the near backs, and the free safety is free.

STUD: Plays 8 technique versus run. Covers the tight end versus pass.

STRONG END: Slants outside and controls the C gap. Contains quarterback versus pass.

STRONG TANDEM: Plays base technique versus run. Covers the near back versus pass.

NOSE: Plays 0 technique versus run. Slants into the strongside A gap versus pass.

MIKE: Plays base technique versus run. Covers the weak back versus pass.

WEAK END: Slants outside and controls the C gap. Contains quarterback versus pass.

WEAK TANDEM: Blitzes through the B gap.

ROVER: Plays 8 technique versus run. Delay blitzes through the weakside A gap versus pass.

FREE SAFETY: Lines up as though he's playing cover 3. Provides alley support to run. Plays centerfield versus pass.

STRONG CORNER: Covers #1. Inside/outside technique dependent upon field position and the distance of flanker's split).

WEAK CORNER: Covers #1. Inside/outside technique dependent upon field position and the distance of split end's split.

STUNT #54

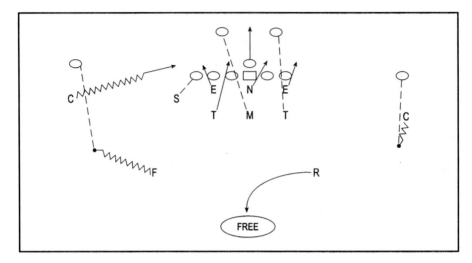

STUNT DESCRIPTION: This is a *dog* that provides the defense with a *strong cornerback blitz*.

SECONDARY COVERAGE: Cover 1 disguised as cover 2. The Stud covers the tight end, Mike and the weak Tandem cover the running backs, and the Rover is free.

STUD: Plays 8 technique versus run. Covers the near back versus pass.

STRONG END: Slants outside and controls the C gap. Contains the quarterback versus pass.

STRONG TANDEM: Blitzes through the B gap.

NOSE: Slants into and controls the weakside A gap.

MIKE: Plays base technique versus run. Covers the strong back versus pass.

WEAK END: Slants outside. Controls the C gap versus run and contains the quarterback versus pass.

WEAK TANDEM: Plays base technique versus run. Covers the weak back versus pass.

ROVER: Plays 8 technique versus run. Drops to centerfield versus pass. Disguises his assignment as cover 2.

FREE SAFETY: Lines up as though he's playing cover 2, but moves to a position that will enable him to cover the flanker during cadence.

STRONG CORNER: Creeps inside during cadence and rushes from the edge. Contains the quarterback and strongside run. Chases weakside run.

WEAK CORNER: Covers the split end. Inside/outside technique dependent upon field position and the distance of split end's split. Disguises his assignment as cover 2.

STUNT #55

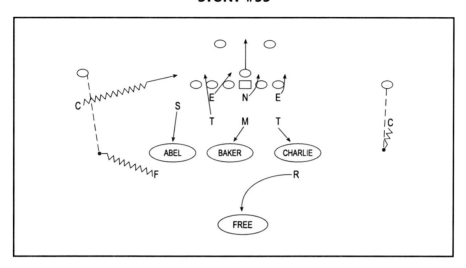

STUNT DESCRIPTION: This *fire zone blitz* provides the defense with a *strong cornerback blitz* and a weakside line slant.

SECONDARY COVERAGE: Cover 1 disguised as cover 2. The Stud, Mike and the weak Tandem drop into coverage, and the Rover is free.

STUD: Plays 8 technique versus run and drops **Abel** versus pass.

STRONG END: Attacks the near shoulder of the offensive guard and secures the B gap.

STRONG TANDEM: Blitzes through the outside shoulder of the offensive tackle and controls the C gap.

NOSE: Slants into and controls the weakside A gap.

MIKE: Plays base technique versus run. Drops **Baker** versus pass.

WEAK END: Slants outside. Controls the C gap versus run and contains the quarterback versus pass.

WEAK TANDEM: Plays base technique versus run. Drops **Charlie** versus pass.

ROVER: Plays 8 technique versus run. Drops to centerfield versus pass. Disguises his assignment as cover 2.

FREE SAFETY: Lines up as though he's playing cover 2, but moves to a position that will enable him to cover the flanker during cadence.

STRONG CORNER: Creeps inside during cadence and rushes from the edge. Contains the quarterback and strongside run. Chases weakside run.

WEAK CORNER: Covers the split end. Inside/outside technique dependent upon field position and the distance of split end's split. Disguises his assignment as cover 2.

STUNT #56

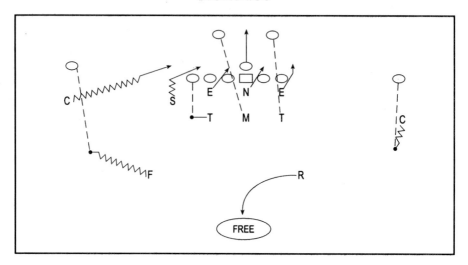

STUNT DESCRIPTION: This *dog* provides the defense with a *strong cornerback blitz*.

SECONDARY COVERAGE: Cover 1 disguised as cover 2. The strong Tandem covers the tight end, the Mike and the weak Tandem cover the running backs, and the Rover is free.

STUD: Creeps toward the line of scrimmage during cadence and rushes from the edge. Contains the quarterback and strongside run. Chases weakside run.

STRONG END: Attacks the near shoulder of the offensive guard and secures the B gap.

STRONG TANDEM: Shuffles outside at the snap and covers the tight end.

NOSE: Slants into and controls the weakside A gap.

MIKE: Plays base technique versus run. Covers the strong back versus pass.

WEAK END: Slants outside. Controls the C gap versus run and contains the quarterback versus pass.

WEAK TANDEM: Plays base technique versus run. Covers the weak back versus pass.

ROVER: Lines up as though he's playing cover 2. Plays 8 technique versus run. Drops to centerfield versus pass.

FREE SAFETY: Lines up as though he's playing cover 2, but moves to a position that will enable him to cover the flanker during cadence.

STRONG CORNER: Creeps inside during cadence and rushes from the edge. Contains the quarterback and strongside run. Chases weakside run.

WEAK CORNER: Covers the split end. Inside/outside technique dependent upon field position and the distance of split end's split. Disguises his assignment as cover 2.

STUNT #57

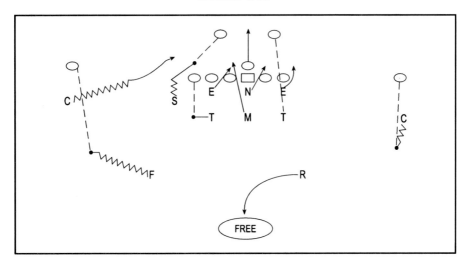

STUNT DESCRIPTION: This *dog* provides the defense with a *strong cornerback blitz* and the illusion of a four-man strongside pass rush.

SECONDARY COVERAGE: Cover 1 disguised as cover 2. The strong Tandem covers the tight end, the Stud and the weak Tandem cover the running backs, and the Rover is free.

STUD: Creeps toward the line of scrimmage during cadence and pretends to rush from the edge. Helps contain strongside run and chases weakside run. Spies the near back versus pass.

STRONG END: Attacks the near shoulder of the offensive guard and secures the B gap.

STRONG TANDEM: Shuffles outside at the snap and covers the tight end.

NOSE: Slants into and controls the weakside A gap.

MIKE: Blitzes through the strongside A gap.

WEAK END: Slants outside. Controls the C gap versus run and contains the quarterback versus pass.

WEAK TANDEM: Plays base technique versus run. Covers the weak back versus pass.

ROVER: Lines up as though he's playing cover 2. Plays 8 technique versus run. Drops to centerfield versus pass.

FREE SAFETY: Lines up as though he's playing cover 2, but moves to a position that will enable him to cover the flanker during cadence.

STRONG CORNER: Creeps inside during cadence and rushes from the edge. Contains the quarterback and strongside run. Chases weakside run.

WEAK CORNER: Covers the split end. Inside/outside technique dependent upon field position and the distance of split end's split. Disguises his assignment as cover 2.

STUNT #58

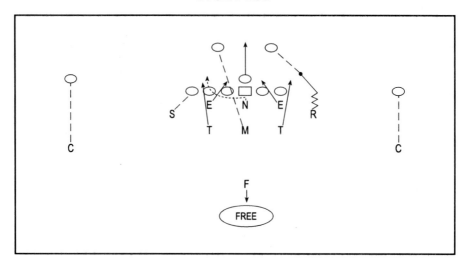

STUNT DESCRIPTION: This is a *dog* that features a *strongside twin stunt*.

SECONDARY COVERAGE: Cover 1. The Stud covers the tight end, Mike and Rover cover the near backs, and the free safety is free.

STUD: Plays 8 technique versus run. Covers the tight end versus pass.

STRONG END: Slants into and quickly penetrates the B gap.

STRONG TANDEM: Blitzes through the outside shoulder of the offensive tackle and controls the C gap. Contains the quarterback versus pass.

NOSE: Plays 0 technique versus run. Loops through the strongside B gap versus pass.

MIKE: Plays base technique versus run. Covers the strong back versus pass.

WEAK END: Slants into and quickly penetrates the B gap.

WEAK TANDEM: Blitzes through the outside shoulder of the offensive tackle and controls the C gap. Contains the quarterback versus pass.

ROVER: Creeps toward the line of scrimmage during cadence and gives impression he will rush from the edge. Contains weakside run and chases strongside run. Spies the near back versus pass.

FREE SAFETY: Lines up as though he's playing cover 3. Provides alley support to run. Plays centerfield versus pass.

STRONG CORNER: Covers #1. Inside/outside technique dependent upon field position and the distance of flanker's split.

WEAK CORNER: Covers #1. Inside/outside technique dependent upon field position and the distance of split end's split.

STUNT #59

STUNT DESCRIPTION: This is a *dog* that provides the defense with excellent pressure from the edge and a *delayed line twist* versus pass.

SECONDARY COVERAGE: Cover 1. The strong Tandem covers the tight end. Mike and the weak Tandem cover the backs, and the free safety is free.

STUD: Creeps toward the line of scrimmage during cadence and rushes from the edge. Contains weakside run and chases strongside run. Contains the quarterback versus pass.

STRONG END: Slants toward and secures the B gap versus run. Continues to slant across the face of the center into the weakside A gap versus pass.

STRONG TANDEM: Shuffles laterally at the snap and covers the tight end.

NOSE: Plays 0 technique versus run. Quickly penetrates the strongside A gap versus pass.

MIKE: Plays base technique versus run. Covers the strong back versus pass.

WEAK END: Slants into and quickly penetrates the B gap.

WEAK TANDEM: Plays base technique versus run. Covers the weak back versus pass.

ROVER: Creeps toward the line of scrimmage during cadence and rushes from the edge. Contains weakside run and chases strongside run. Contains the quarterback versus pass.

FREE SAFETY: Lines up as though he's playing cover 3. Provides alley support to run. Plays centerfield versus pass.

STRONG CORNER: Covers #1. Inside/outside technique dependent upon field position and the distance of flanker's split.

WEAK CORNER: Covers #1. Inside/outside technique dependent upon field position and the distance of split end's split.

STUNT #60

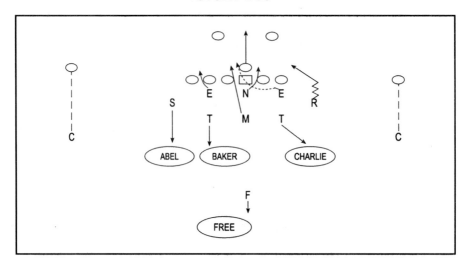

STUNT DESCRIPTION: This is a *fire zone blitz* that features a delayed line twist that results in a twin stunt.

SECONDARY COVERAGE: Cover 1. The Tandems and Stud drop into coverage and the free safety is free.

STUD: Plays 8 technique versus run. Drops **Abel** versus pass.

STRONG END: Slants into and controls the C gap. Contains the quarterback versus pass.

STRONG TANDEM: Plays base technique versus run. Drops **Baker** versus pass.

NOSE: Quickly penetrates the weakside A gap.

MIKE: Blitzes through the strongside A gap.

WEAK END: Slants toward and secures the B gap versus run. Continues to slant across the face of the center into the strongside A gap versus pass.

WEAK TANDEM: Plays base technique versus run. Drops **Charlie** versus pass.

ROVER: Creeps toward the line of scrimmage during cadence and rushes from the edge. Contains the quarterback and weakside run. Chases strongside run.

FREE SAFETY: Lines up as though he's playing cover 3. Provides alley support to run. Plays centerfield versus pass.

STRONG CORNER: Covers #1. Inside/outside technique dependent upon field position and the distance of flanker's split.

WEAK CORNER: Covers #1. Inside/outside technique dependent upon field position and the distance of split end's split.

STUNT #61

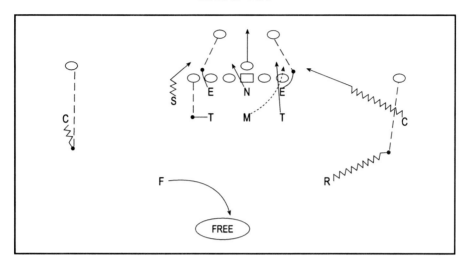

STUNT DESCRIPTION: This is a *dog* provides the defense with a weak cornerback blitz and a *delayed linebacker blitz.*

SECONDARY COVERAGE: Cover 1 disguised as cover 2. The strong Tandem covers the tight end, the ends spy the running backs, and the free safety is free.

STUD: Creeps toward the line of scrimmage during cadence and rushes from the edge. Contains the quarterback and strongside run. Chases weakside run.

STRONG END: Slants outside and controls the C gap. Spies the near back versus pass.

STRONG TANDEM: Shuffles outside at the snap and covers the tight end.

NOSE: Slants into and controls the strongside A gap.

MIKE: Plays base technique versus run. Blitzes through the weakside B gap versus pass.

WEAK END: Slants outside. Controls the C gap versus run and spies the near back versus pass.

WEAK TANDEM: Blitzes through the B gap. Quick penetration of this gap is vital.

ROVER: Lines up as though he's playing cover 2, but moves to a position that will enable him to cover the split end when the ball is snapped.

FREE SAFETY: Lines up as though he's playing cover 2. Provides alley support to run and drops to centerfield versus pass.

STRONG CORNER: Lines up as though he's playing cover 2. Covers the flanker. Inside/outside technique dependent upon field position and the distance of flanker's split.

WEAK CORNER: Lines up as though he's playing cover 2. Creeps inside during cadence and rushes from the edge. Contains the quarterback and weakside run. Chases strongside run.

STUNT #62

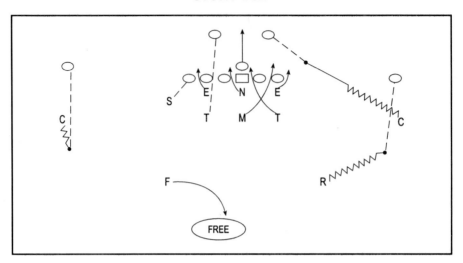

STUNT DESCRIPTION: This is a *dog* provides the defense with a fake weak cornerback blitz.

SECONDARY COVERAGE: Cover 1 disguised as cover 2. The Stud covers the tight end, the strong Tandem and weak cornerback cover the running backs, and the free safety is free.

STUD: Plays 8 technique versus run. Covers the tight end versus pass.

STRONG END: Slants outside and controls the C gap. Contains the quarterback versus pass.

STRONG TANDEM: Plays base technique versus run. Covers the near back versus pass.

NOSE: Slants into and controls the strongside A gap.

MIKE: Blitzes through the weakside B gap. He will blitz behind the weak tandem. His fist step should thus be parallel to the line with his right foot.

WEAK END: Slants outside. Controls the C gap versus run and contains the quarterback versus pass.

WEAK TANDEM: Blitzes through the A gap. He goes first.

ROVER: Lines up as though he's playing cover 2, but moves to a position that will enable him to cover the split end when the ball is snapped.

FREE SAFETY: Lines up as though he's playing cover 2. Provides alley support to run and drops to centerfield versus pass.

STRONG CORNER: Lines up as though he's playing cover 2. Covers the flanker. Inside/outside technique dependent upon field position and the distance of flanker's split.

WEAK CORNER: Lines up as though he's playing cover 2. Creeps inside during cadence and gives impression he will rush from the edge. Contains weakside run and chases strongside run. Spies the near back versus pass.

STUNT #63

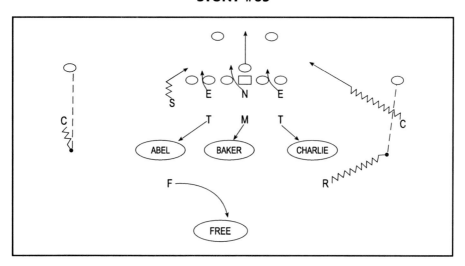

STUNT DESCRIPTION: This is a *fire zone blitz* that provides the defense with a weak cornerback blitz.

SECONDARY COVERAGE: Cover 1 disguised as cover 2. The strong Tandem, Mike, and the weak tandem drop into coverage, and the free safety is free.

STUD: Creeps toward the line during cadence and rushes from the edge. Contains the quarterback and strongside run. Chases weakside run.

STRONG END: Slants outside and controls the C gap.

STRONG TANDEM: Plays base technique versus run. Drops **Abel** versus pass.

NOSE: Slants into and controls the strongside A gap.

MIKE: Plays base technique versus run. Drops **Baker** versus pass.

WEAK END: Slants into and controls the B gap.

WEAK TANDEM: Plays base technique versus run. Drops **Charlie** versus pass.

ROVER: Lines up as though he's playing cover 2, but moves to a position that will enable him to cover the split end when the ball is snapped.

FREE SAFETY: Lines up as though he's playing cover 2. Provides alley support to run and drops to centerfield versus pass.

STRONG CORNER: Line up as though he's playing cover 2. Covers the flanker. Inside/outside technique dependent upon field position and the distance of flanker's split.

WEAK CORNER: Lines up as though he's playing cover 2. Creeps inside during cadence and rushes from the edge. Contains the quarterback and weakside run. Chases strongside run.

STUNT #64

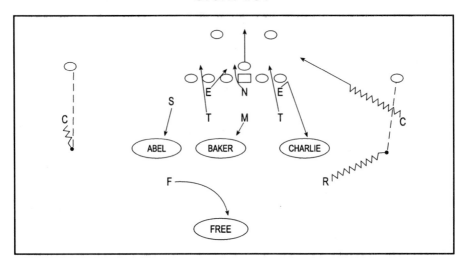

STUNT DESCRIPTION: This is another *fire zone blitz* that provides the defense with a weak cornerback blitz and drops a defensive lineman into coverage.

SECONDARY COVERAGE: Cover 1 disguised as cover 2. Stud, Mike, and the weak end drop into coverage, and the free safety is free.

STUD: Plays 8 technique versus run. Drops **Abel** versus pass.

STRONG END: Slants into and controls the B gap.

STRONG TANDEM: Blitzes through the outside shoulder of the offensive tackle and secures the C gap against run. Contains the quarterback versus pass.

NOSE: Slants into and controls the strongside A gap.

MIKE: Plays base technique versus run. Drops **Baker** versus pass.

WEAK END: Slants outside and secures the C gap versus run. Drops **Charlie** versus pass.

WEAK TANDEM: Blitzes through the B gap.

ROVER: Lines up as though he's playing cover 2, but moves to a position that will enable him to cover the split end when the ball is snapped.

FREE SAFETY: Lines up as though he's playing cover 2. Provides alley support to run and drops to centerfield versus pass.

STRONG CORNER: Lines up as though he's playing cover 2. Covers the flanker. Inside/outside technique dependent upon field position and the distance of flanker's split.

WEAK CORNER: Lines up as though he's playing cover 2. Creeps inside during cadence and rushes from the edge. Contains the quarterback and weakside run. Chases strongside run.

5

Cover 3 Stunts

The following pattern read guidelines will assist defenders who drop into one of the cover 3 zones.

Strong Hook-Curl Drop

The defender should:

- Drop into the strong hook zone to a depth of 12-15 yards
- Key #2 (the tight end).
- Stay in the hook and collision #2 if he runs a vertical route.
- Sprint to the curl and look for #1 (the flanker) to run a curl or a post if #2 releases into the flats.
- Try to collision#2 if he runs inside and across the defender's face, and then look for another receiver to run a crossing route into the defender's zone.

Weak Hook-Curl Drop

The defender should:

- Open up and drop into the weak hook zone to a depth of 12-15 yards and key #2 (the weakside halfback).
- Stay in the hook zone and collision #2 if he runs a vertical route.

- Sprint to the curl and look for #1 (the split end) to run a curl or a post if #2 releases into the flats
- If #2 runs inside and across your face, try to collision #2 if he runs inside and across the defender's face, and then look for another receiver to run a crossing route into the defender's zone.

Strong Curl-Out Drop

The defender should:

- Open up and drop to a depth of 10-12 yards.
- Find an aiming point three yards inside of where #1 (the flanker) is lined up.
- Key #1.
- Try to get into the throwing lane and get a piece of the ball if #1 runs an out.
- Stay inside of #1's pattern if he runs a curl or a post and check #2 (the tight end).
- Release from #1's curl or post if #2 crosses the defender's face while running an out.
- Sink and check #2 and #3 if #1 runs a vertical route.

Weak Curl-Out Drop

The defender should:

- Open up and drop to a depth of 10-12 yards.
- Find an aiming point three yards inside of where #1 (the split end) is lined up.
- Key #1.
- Try to get into the throwing lane and get a piece of the ball if #1 runs an out.
- Stay inside of #1's pattern if he runs a curl or a post and check #2 (the weakside halfback).
- Release from #1's curl or post when #2 crosses the defender's face while running an out.
- Sink and check #2 if #1 runs a vertical route.

Deep Outside Third Drop

The defender should:

- See both #1 and #2 as he backpedals.
- Stay as deep as the deepest receiver in his zone.
- Look for #2 to threaten deep if #1 runs a short or intermediate route.
- Control the speed of his backpedal so that he can break on the ball if #2 also runs a short or intermediate route.

- Maintain a cushion of 3-4 yards if #1 runs a vertical route.
- Stay on #1's outside hip and maintain a sufficient cushion if he runs a post.

Deep Middle Third Drop

A defensive back should:

- Drop midway between the two cornerbacks, stay as deep as the deepest receiver, and play center field.
- Key #2's release. If it is vertical, the defender must get into a position to cover it. If #2's route is short, the defender checks the split end and flanker for the post pattern.

Adjusting Cover 3 to Offensive Formations

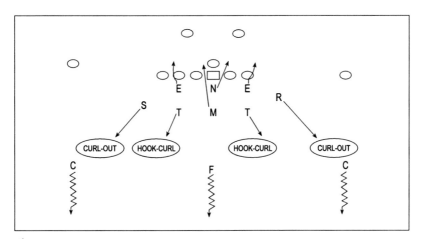

Figure 5-1a

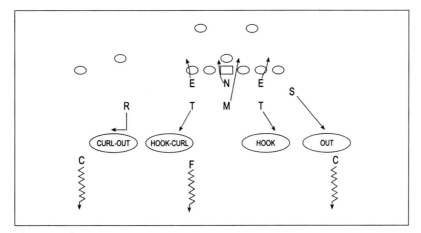

Figure 5-1b

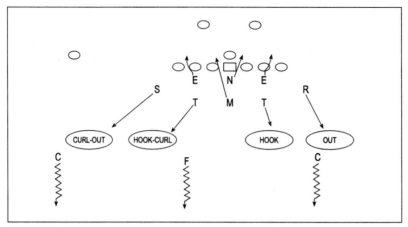

Figure 5-1c

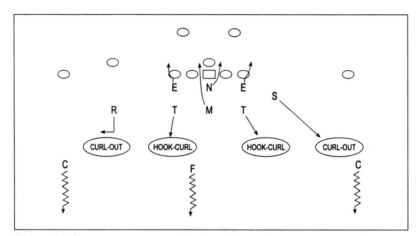

Figure 5-1d

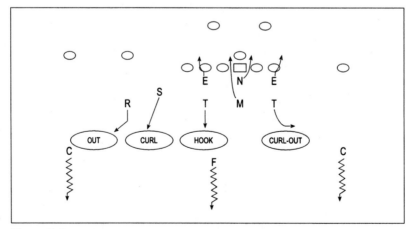

Figure 5-1e

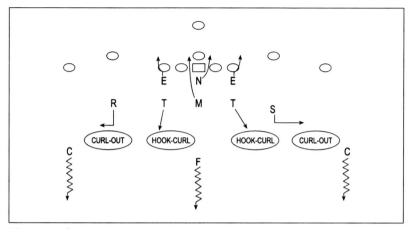

Figure 5-1f

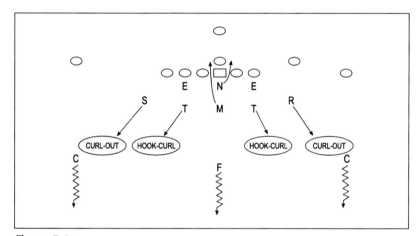

Figure 5-1g

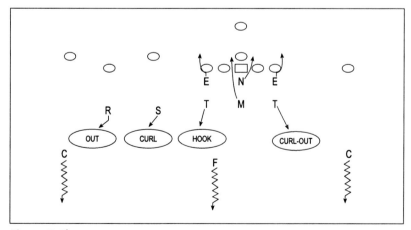

Figure 5-1h

STUNT #65

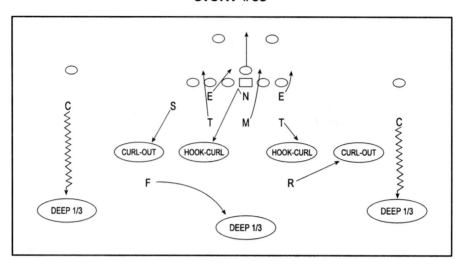

STUNT DESCRIPTION: This is an *old school zone blitz*.

SECONDARY COVERAGE: Cover 3 disguised as cover 2. The Stud, Nose, Rover, and the weak tandem drop into coverage.

STUD: Plays 8 technique versus run. Drops curl-out versus pass.

STRONG END: Attacks the near shoulder of the offensive guard and controls the B gap.

STRONG TANDEM: Blitzes through the outside shoulder of the offensive tackle and secures the C gap versus run. Contains the quarterback versus pass.

NOSE: Slants to and secures the strongside A gap versus run. Drops hook-curl versus pass.

MIKE: Blitzes through the weakside A gap.

WEAK END: Slants outside, controls the C gap, and contains the quarterback.

WEAK TANDEM: Plays base technique versus run. Drops hook-curl versus pass.

ROVER: Lines up as though he's playing cover 2. Plays 8 technique versus run. Drops curl-out versus pass.

FREE SAFETY: Lines up as though he's playing cover 2. Provides alley support to run and covers the deep middle third versus pass.

STRONG CORNER: Lines up as though he's playing cover 2. Covers the deep outside third.

WEAK CORNER: Lines up as though he's playing cover 2. Covers the deep outside third.

STUNT #66

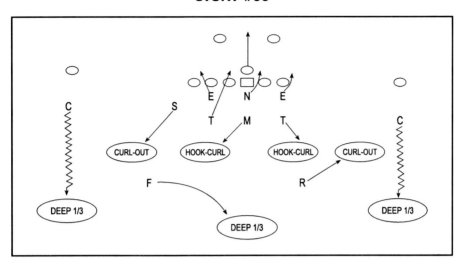

STUNT DESCRIPTION: This stunt sends the strong Tandem.

SECONDARY COVERAGE: Cover 3 disguised as cover 2. The Stud, Mike, Rover, and the weak tandem drop into coverage.

STUD: Plays 8 technique versus run. Drops curl-out versus pass.

STRONG END: Slants outside, controls the C gap and contains the quarterback.

STRONG TANDEM: Blitzes through the B gap.

NOSE: Slants into and controls the weakside A gap.

MIKE: Plays base technique versus run. Drops hook-curl versus pass.

WEAK END: Slants outside, controls the C gap, and contains the quarterback.

WEAK TANDEM: Plays base technique versus run. Drops hook-curl versus pass.

ROVER: Lines up as though he's playing cover 2. Plays 8 technique versus run. Drops curl-out versus pass.

FREE SAFETY: Lines up as though he's playing cover 2. Provides alley support to run and cover the deep middle third versus pass.

STRONG CORNER: Lines up as though he's playing cover 2. Covers the deep outside third.

WEAK CORNER: Lines up as though he's playing cover 2. Covers the deep outside third.

STUNT #67

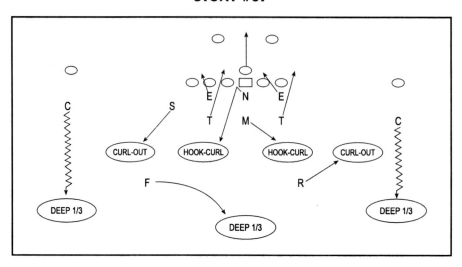

STUNT DESCRIPTION: This is an *old school zone blitz*.

SECONDARY COVERAGE: Cover 3 disguised as cover 2. The Stud, Nose, Mike, and Rover drop into coverage.

STUD: Plays 8 technique versus run. Drops curl-out versus pass.

STRONG END: Slants outside, controls the C gap and contains the quarterback.

STRONG TANDEM: Blitzes through the outside shoulder of the offensive guard and controls the B gap.

NOSE: Slants to and secures the strongside A gap versus run. Drops hook-curl versus pass.

MIKE: Plays base technique versus run. Drops hook-curl versus pass.

WEAK END: Attacks the near shoulder of the offensive guard and controls the B gap.

WEAK TANDEM: Blitzes through the outside shoulder of the offensive tackle, controls the C gap, and contains the quarterback.

ROVER: Lines up as though he's playing cover 2. Plays 8 technique versus run. Drops curl-out versus pass.

FREE SAFETY: Lines up as though he's playing cover 2. Provides alley support to run and covers the deep middle third versus pass.

STRONG CORNER: Lines up as though he's playing cover 2. Covers the deep outside third.

WEAK CORNER: Lines up as though he's playing cover 2. Covers the deep outside third.

STUNT #68

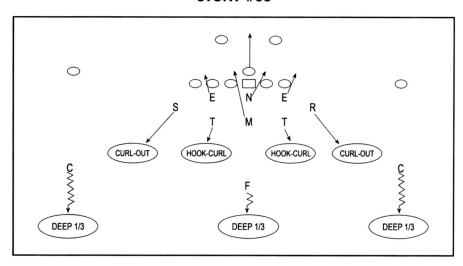

STUNT DESCRIPTION: This is an *old school zone blitz*. Most 3-5 teams use it as their base defense.

SECONDARY COVERAGE: Cover 3. The Stud, Rover, and tandems drop into coverage.

STUD: Plays 8 technique versus run. Drops curl-out versus pass.

STRONG END: Slants outside, controls the C gap and contains the quarterback.

STRONG TANDEM: Plays base technique versus run. Drops hook-curl versus pass.

NOSE: Slants into the weakside A gap.

MIKE: Blitzes through the strongside A gap.

WEAK END: Slants outside, controls the C gap and contains the quarterback.

WEAK TANDEM: Plays base technique versus run. Drops hook-curl versus pass.

ROVER: Plays 8 technique versus run. Drops curl-out versus pass.

FREE SAFETY: Provides alley support to run and covers the deep middle third versus pass.

STRONG CORNER: Covers the deep outside third.

WEAK CORNER: Cover the deep outside third.

STUNT #69

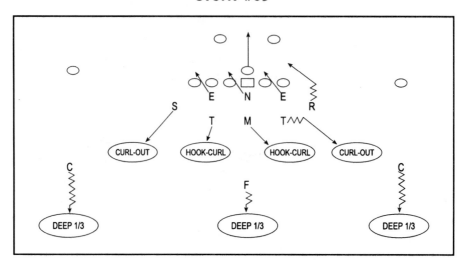

STUNT DESCRIPTION: This strongside line slant provides the defense with excellent armament versus the run. This stunt is best called when the ball is on the hash and the strength of the formation is aligned to the wide side of the field.

SECONDARY COVERAGE: Cover 3. The Stud, Mike, and Tandems drop into coverage.

STUD: Plays 8 technique versus run. Drops curl-out versus pass.

STRONG END: Slants outside, controls the C gap and contains the quarterback.

STRONG TANDEM: Plays base technique versus run. Drops hook-curl versus pass.

NOSE: Slants into the strongside A gap.

MIKE: Plays base technique versus run. Drops hook-curl versus pass.

WEAK END: Attacks the near shoulder of the offensive guard and controls the B gap.

WEAK TANDEM: Plays base technique versus run. Drops curl-out versus pass.

ROVER: Creeps toward the line of scrimmage during cadence and rushes from the edge. Contains the quarterback and weakside run. Chases strongside run.

FREE SAFETY: Provides alley support to run and covers the deep middle third versus pass.

STRONG CORNER: Covers the deep outside third.

WEAK CORNER: Covers the deep outside third.

STUNT #70

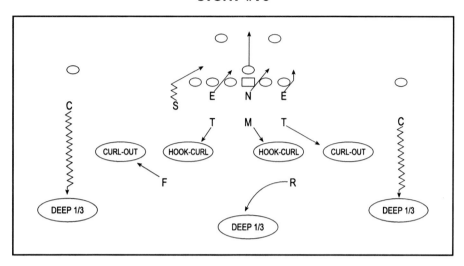

STUNT DESCRIPTION: This stunt is best called when the ball is on the hash and the strength of the formation is aligned to the wide side of the field. Provides the defense with a rotating invert concept that is particularly effective versus the option.

SECONDARY COVERAGE: Cover 3 disguised as cover 2. The Tandems, Mike and the free safety drop into coverage.

STUD: Creeps toward the line of scrimmage during cadence and rushes from the edge. Contains the quarterback and strongside run. Chases weakside run.

STRONG END: Attacks the near shoulder of the offensive guard and controls the B gap.

STRONG TANDEM: Plays base technique versus run. Drops hook-curl versus pass.

NOSE: Slants into the weakside A gap.

MIKE: Plays base technique versus run. Drops hook-curl versus pass.

WEAK END: Slants outside, controls the C gap, and contains the quarterback.

WEAK TANDEM: Plays base technique versus run. Drops curl-out versus pass.

ROVER: Lines up as though he's playing cover 2. Contains weakside run. Drops to centerfield versus pass and strongside run.

FREE SAFETY: Lines up as though he's playing cover 2. Helps contain strongside run. Drops to centerfield versus pass and weakside run.

STRONG CORNER: Lines up as though he's playing cover 2. Covers the deep outside third.

WEAK CORNER: Lines up as though he's playing cover 2. Covers the deep outside third.

STUNT #71

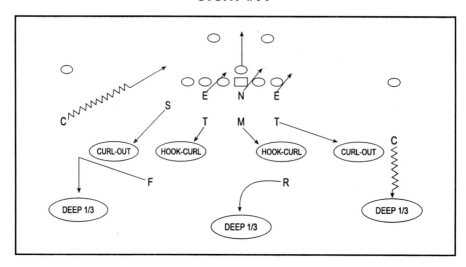

STUNT DESCRIPTION: This stunt provides the defense with a strong cornerback blitz.

SECONDARY COVERAGE: Cover 3 disguised as cover 2. The Tandems, Mike, and Stud drop into coverage.

STUD: Plays 8 technique versus run. Drops curl-out versus pass.

STRONG END: Attacks the near shoulder of the offensive guard and controls the B gap.

STRONG TANDEM: Plays base technique versus run. Drops hook-curl versus pass.

NOSE: Slants into the weakside A gap.

MIKE: Plays base technique versus run. Drops hook-curl versus pass.

WEAK END: Slants outside, controls the C gap, and contains the quarterback.

WEAK TANDEM: Plays base technique versus run. Drops curl-out versus pass.

ROVER: Lines up as though he's playing cover 2 and drops to centerfield versus pass. He is responsible for deep middle third.

FREE SAFETY: Lines up as though he's playing cover 2 but moves to a position that will enable him to cover deep outside third when the ball is snapped.

STRONG CORNER: Lines up as though he's playing cover 2, but creeps inside during cadence and rushes from the edge. Contains the quarterback and strongside run. Chases weakside run.

WEAK CORNER: Covers the deep outside third. Disguises his assignment as cover 2.

STUNT #72

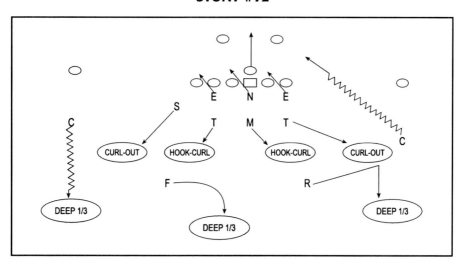

STUNT DESCRIPTION: This stunt provides the defense with a weak cornerback blitz.

SECONDARY COVERAGE: Cover 3 disguised as cover 2. The Tandems, Mike and Stud drop into coverage.

STUD: Plays 8 technique versus run. Drops curl-out versus pass.

STRONG END: Slants outside, controls the C gap and contains the quarterback.

STRONG TANDEM: Plays base technique versus run. Drops hook-curl versus pass.

NOSE: Slants into the strongside A gap.

MIKE: Plays base technique versus run. Drops hook-curl versus pass.

WEAK END: Attacks the near shoulder of the offensive guard and controls the B gap.

WEAK TANDEM: Plays base technique versus run. Drops curl-out versus pass.

ROVER: Lines up as though he's playing cover 2 but moves to a position that will enable him to cover deep outside third when the ball is snapped.

FREE SAFETY: Lines up as though he's playing cover 2 and drops to centerfield versus pass. He is responsible for deep middle third.

STRONG CORNER: Covers the deep outside third. Disguises his assignment as cover 2.

WEAK CORNER: Lines up as though he's playing cover 2, but creeps inside during cadence and rushes from the edge. Contains the quarterback and weakside run. Chases strongside run.

Cover 2 Zone Stunts

In Chapter 4 the cover 3 pattern reads and drop assignments for defenders in the underneath zones were explained in detail. Those reads and assignments are identical to the reads and assignments of cover 2 zone. Before presenting the cover 2 zone stunts, this chapter begins with some explanations of the assignments, techniques and pattern reads for the two defenders in deep half coverage.

Assignments and Reads for Deep Half Coverage

A defender should:

- Stay as deep as the deepest receiver.
- Communicate routes to defenders dropping into the underneath zones.
- Read receivers #1 and #2. Work toward and maintain an adequate cushion on the deepest receiver.
- Move outside of #2, if both receivers go deep, so that he will be able to break to #1.
- If #2 releases into the flats, gain width and depth. Put himself in a position to react to the route being run by #1.
- If #2 releases inside, gain width and look first to #1 and then to a deep crossing route.

Cornerback's Cover 2 Technique

A defender should:

- Jam receiver #1. Stay on his outside shoulder and funnel him inside. Do not allow #1 an outside release.
- If #1 runs a vertical route, continue to funnel his pattern inside. The defender should also continue to gain depth as long as there is no immediate threat in the flats.
- As the defender funnels #1 inside, he should see the release of receiver #2.
- If #2 releases short and into the flat, gain depth and width. The defender should not react to #2 until he crosses the defender's face.
- If #2 runs the wheel route, collision and run with him.
- If #2 runs a vertical or crossing route, stay with #1 unless threatened by #3. If #3 releases into the flats, the defender must be in a position to rally up.

Adjusting Cover 2 Zone to Offensive Formations

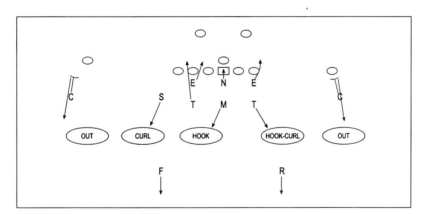

Figure 6-1a

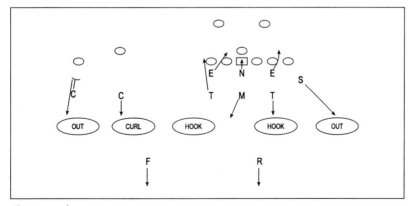

Figure 6-1b

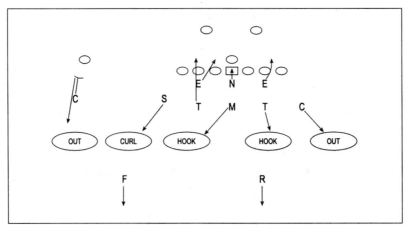

Figure 6-1c

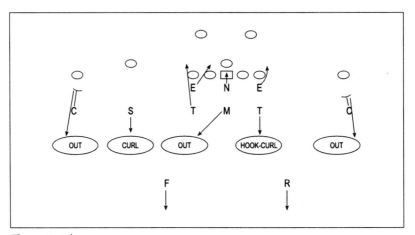

Figure 6-1d

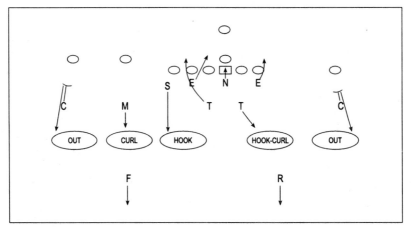

Figure 6-1e

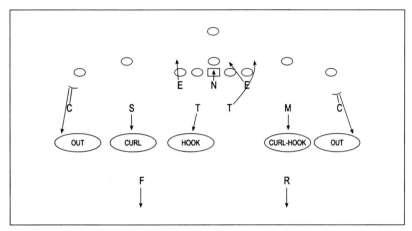

Figure 6-1f

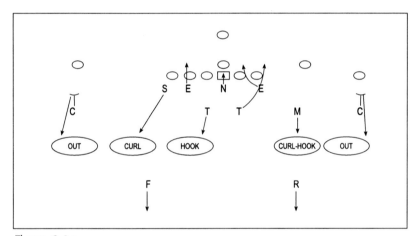

Figure 6-1g

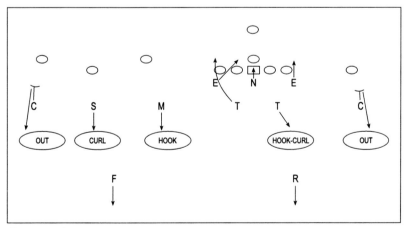

Figure 6-1h

STUNT #73

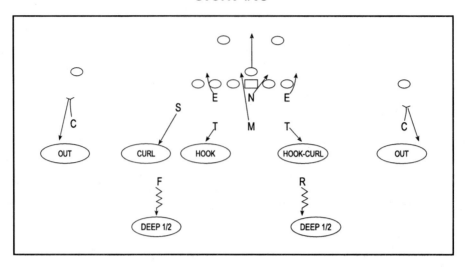

STUNT DESCRIPTION: This is a simple *stunt* that sends Mike. Most 3-5 teams will use it as their base cover 2 stunt.

SECONDARY COVERAGE: Cover 2 zone. The Stud and the Tandems drop into coverage.

STUD: Plays 8 technique versus run. Drops curl versus pass.

STRONG END: Slants outside, controls the C gap, and contains the quarterback.

STRONG TANDEM: Plays base technique versus run. Drops hook versus pass.

NOSE: Slants into and controls the weakside A gap.

MIKE: Blitzes through the strongside A gap.

WEAK END: Slants outside, controls the C gap, and contains the quarterback.

WEAK TANDEM: Plays base technique versus run. Drops hook-curl versus pass.

ROVER: Covers the deep half of the field.

FREE SAFETY: Covers the deep half of the field.

STRONG CORNER: Funnels the flanker inside and covers the out.

WEAK CORNER: Funnels the flanker inside and covers the out.

STUNT #74

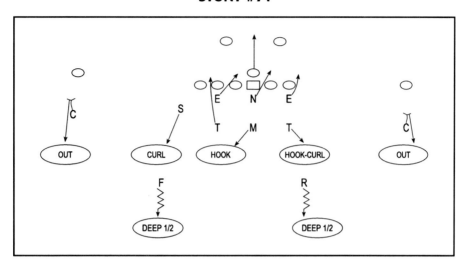

STUNT DESCRIPTION: This is a *stunt* sends the strong Tandem and is enhanced by a weakside line slant.

SECONDARY COVERAGE: Cover 2 zone. Stud, Mike and the weak Tandem drop into coverage.

STUD: Plays 8 technique versus run. Drops curl versus pass.

STRONG END: Attacks the near shoulder of the offensive guard and controls the B gap.

STRONG TANDEM: Blitzes through the outside shoulder of the offensive tackle, controls the C gap, and contains the quarterback.

NOSE: Slants into and controls the weakside A gap.

MIKE: Plays base technique versus run. Drops hook versus pass.

WEAK END: Slants outside, controls the C gap, and contains the quarterback.

WEAK TANDEM: Plays base technique versus run. Drops hook-curl versus pass.

ROVER: Covers the deep half of the field.

FREE SAFETY: Covers the deep half of the field.

STRONG CORNER: Funnels the flanker inside and covers the out.

WEAK CORNER: Funnels the flanker inside and covers the out.

STUNT #75

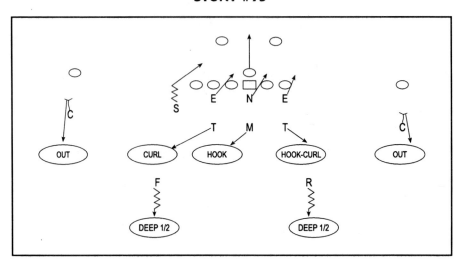

STUNT DESCRIPTION: This is a *stunt* that sends Stud and is enhanced by a weakside line slant.

SECONDARY COVERAGE: Cover 2 zone. The Tandems and Mike drop into coverage.

STUD: Creeps toward the line of scrimmage during cadence and rushes from the edge. Contains the quarterback and strongside run. Chases weakside run.

STRONG END: Attacks the near shoulder of the offensive guard and controls the B gap.

STRONG TANDEM: Plays base technique versus run. Drops curl versus pass.

NOSE: Slants into and controls the weakside A gap.

MIKE: Plays base technique versus run. Drops hook versus pass.

WEAK END: Slants outside, controls the C gap, and contains the quarterback.

WEAK TANDEM: Plays base technique versus run. Drops hook-curl versus pass.

ROVER: Covers the deep half of the field.

FREE SAFETY: Covers the deep half of the field.

STRONG CORNER: Funnels the flanker inside and covers the out.

WEAK CORNER: Funnels the flanker inside and covers the out.

STUNT #76

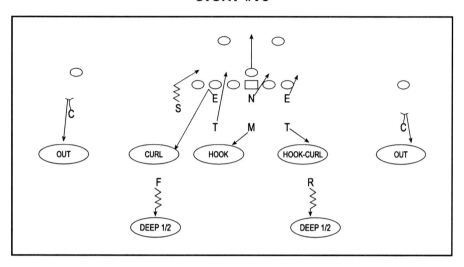

STUNT DESCRIPTION: This is an *old school zone blitz* that drops the strong end into coverage.

SECONDARY COVERAGE: Cover 2 zone. The Mike, the strong end and weak Tandem drop into coverage.

STUD: Creeps toward the line of scrimmage during cadence and rushes from the edge. Contains the quarterback and strongside run. Chases weakside run.

STRONG END: Slants outside, and controls the C gap. Drops curl versus pass.

STRONG TANDEM: Blitzes through the outside shoulder of the offensive guard and controls the B gap.

NOSE: Slants into and controls the weakside A gap.

MIKE: Plays base technique versus run. Drops hook versus pass.

WEAK END: Slants outside, controls the C gap, and contains the quarterback.

WEAK TANDEM: Plays base technique versus run. Drops hook-curl versus pass.

ROVER: Covers the deep half of the field.

FREE SAFETY: Cover the deep half of the field.

STRONG CORNER: Funnels the flanker inside and covers the out.

WEAK CORNER: Funnels the flanker inside and covers the out.

STUNT #77

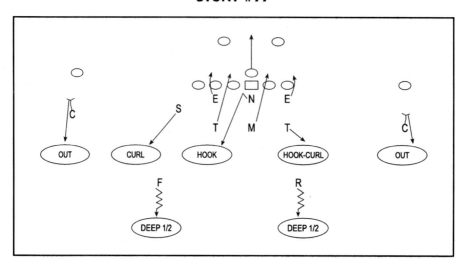

STUNT DESCRIPTION: This is an *old school zone blitz* that drops the Nose into coverage.

SECONDARY COVERAGE: Cover 2 zone. Stud, the Nose and weak Tandem drop into coverage.

STUD: Plays 8 technique versus run. Drops curl versus pass.

STRONG END: Slants outside, controls the C gap, and contains the quarterback.

STRONG TANDEM: Blitzes through the outside shoulder of the offensive guard and controls the B gap.

NOSE: Slants to and controls the strongside A gap. Drops hook versus pass.

MIKE: Blitzes through and controls the strongside A gap.

WEAK END: Slants outside, controls the C gap, and contains the quarterback.

WEAK TANDEM: Plays base technique versus run. Drops hook-curl versus pass.

ROVER: Covers the deep half of the field.

FREE SAFETY: Covers the deep half of the field.

STRONG CORNER: Funnels the flanker inside and covers the out.

WEAK CORNER: Funnels the flanker inside and covers the out.

STUNT #78

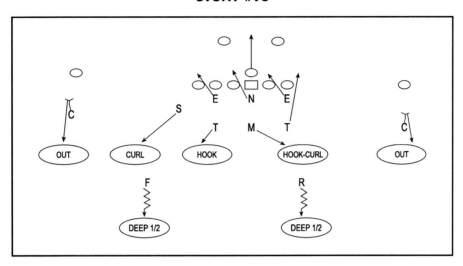

STUNT DESCRIPTION: This *stunt* sends the weak Tandem and provides the defense with a strongside line slant.

SECONDARY COVERAGE: Cover 2 zone. Stud, Mike and the strong Tandem drop into coverage.

STUD: Plays 8 technique versus run. Drops curl versus pass.

STRONG END: Slants outside, controls the C gap, and contains the quarterback.

STRONG TANDEM: Plays base technique versus run. Drops hook versus pass.

NOSE: Slants to and controls the strongside A gap.

MIKE: Plays base technique versus run. Drops hook-curl versus pass.

WEAK END: Attacks the near shoulder of the offensive guard and controls the B gap.

WEAK TANDEM: Blitzes through the outside shoulder of the offensive tackle, controls the C gap, and contains the quarterback .

ROVER: Covers the deep half of the field.

FREE SAFETY: Covers the deep half of the field.

STRONG CORNER: Funnels the flanker inside and covers the out.

WEAK CORNER: Funnels the flanker inside and covers the out.

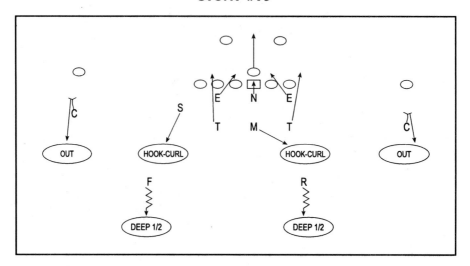

STUNT DESCRIPTION: This is a *dog*.

SECONDARY COVERAGE: A variation of cover 2 zone that drops only four defenders into the under coverage. The Stud and Mike drop into coverage.

STUD: Plays 8 technique versus run. Drops hook-curl versus pass.

STRONG END: Attacks the near shoulder of the offensive guard and controls the B gap.

STRONG TANDEM: Blitzes through the outside shoulder of the offensive tackle, controls the C gap, and contains the quarterback.

NOSE: Plays 0 technique.

MIKE: Plays base technique versus run. Drops hook-curl versus pass.

WEAK END: Attacks the near shoulder of the offensive guard and controls the B gap.

WEAK TANDEM: Blitzes through the outside shoulder of the offensive tackle, controls the C gap and contains the quarterback.

ROVER: Covers the deep half of the field.

FREE SAFETY: Covers the deep half of the field.

STRONG CORNER: Funnels the flanker inside and covers the out.

WEAK CORNER: Funnels the flanker inside and covers the out.

STUNT #80

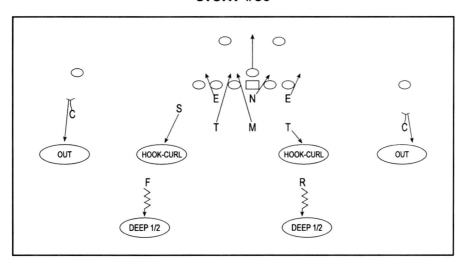

STUNT DESCRIPTION: This is a *dog*.

SECONDARY COVERAGE: A variation of cover 2 Zone that drops only four defenders into the under coverage. The Stud and the weak Tandem drop into coverage.

STUD: Plays 8 technique versus run. Drops hook-curl versus pass.

STRONG END: Slants outside, controls the C gap, and contains the quarterback.

STRONG TANDEM: Blitzes through the outside shoulder of the offensive guard and controls the B gap.

NOSE: Slants to and controls the weakside A gap.

MIKE: Blitzes through the strongside A gap.

WEAK END: Slants outside, controls the C gap, and contains the quarterback.

WEAK TANDEM: Plays base technique versus run. Drops hook-curl versus pass.

ROVER: Covers the deep half of the field.

FREE SAFETY: Covers the deep half of the field.

STRONG CORNER: Funnels the flanker inside and covers the out.

WEAK CORNER: Funnels the flanker inside and covers the out.

STUNT #81

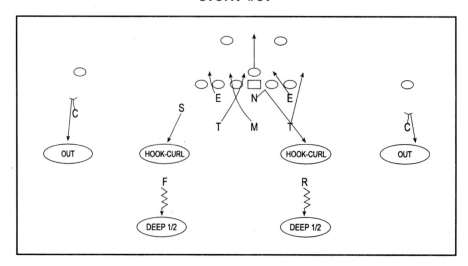

STUNT DESCRIPTION: This is a *dog* that incorporates *old school zone blitz* principles into its scheme.

SECONDARY COVERAGE: A variation of cover 2 Zone that drops only four defenders into the under coverage. Stud and Nose drop into coverage.

STUD: Plays 8 technique versus run. Drops hook-curl versus pass.

STRONG END: Slants outside, controls the C gap, and contains the quarterback.

STRONG TANDEM: Blitzes through the strongside A gap. Mike goes first.

NOSE: Slants to and controls the weakside A gap. Drops hook-curl versus pass.

MIKE: Blitzes through the strongside B gap. He goes first.

WEAK END: Attacks the near shoulder of the offensive guard and controls the B gap.

WEAK TANDEM: Blitzes through the outside shoulder of the offensive tackle, controls the C gap, and contains the quarterback.

ROVER: Covers the deep half of the field.

FREE SAFETY: Covers the deep half of the field.

STRONG CORNER: Funnels the flanker inside and covers the out.

WEAK CORNER: Funnels the flanker inside and covers the out.

STUNT #82

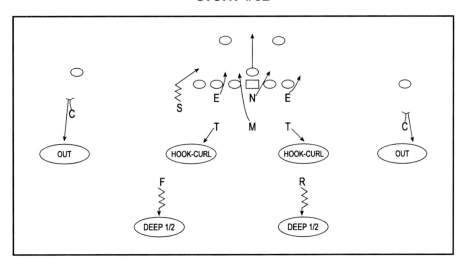

STUNT DESCRIPTION: This is a *dog* that affords the defense excellent strongside pressure from the edge and a weakside line slant.

SECONDARY COVERAGE: A variation of cover 2 zone that drops only four defenders into the under coverage. The Tandems drop into coverage.

STUD: Creeps toward the line of scrimmage during cadence and rushes from the edge. Contains the quarterback and strongside run. Chases weakside run.

STRONG END: Attacks the near shoulder of the offensive guard and controls the B gap.

STRONG TANDEM: Plays base technique versus run. Drops hook-curl versus pass.

NOSE: Slants to and controls the weakside A gap.

MIKE: Blitzes through the strongside A gap.

WEAK END: Slants outside, controls the C gap, and contains the quarterback.

WEAK TANDEM: Plays base technique versus run. Drops hook-curl versus pass.

ROVER: Covers the deep half of the field.

FREE SAFETY: Covers the deep half of the field.

STRONG CORNER: Funnels the flanker inside and covers the out.

WEAK CORNER: Funnels the flanker inside and covers the out.

STUNT #83

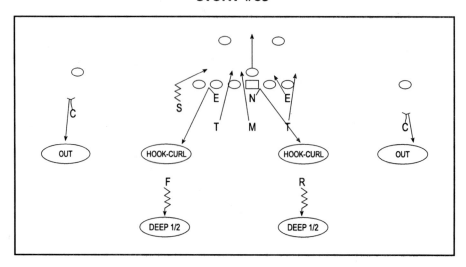

STUNT DESCRIPTION: This is a *dog* that incorporates *old school zone blitz* principles into its scheme.

SECONDARY COVERAGE: A variation of cover 2 Zone that drops only four defenders into the under coverage. The strong end and Nose drop into coverage.

STUD: Creeps toward the line of scrimmage during cadence and rushes from the edge. Contains the quarterback and strongside run. Chases weakside run.

STRONG END: Slants outside and controls the C gap. Drops hook-curl versus pass.

STRONG TANDEM: Blitzes through the strong outside shoulder of the offensive guard and controls the B gap.

NOSE: Slants to and controls the weakside A gap. Drops hook-curl versus pass.

MIKE: Blitzes through the strongside A gap.

WEAK END: Attacks the near shoulder of the offensive guard and controls the B gap.

WEAK TANDEM: Blitzes through the outside shoulder of the offensive tackle, controls the C gap, and contains the quarterback.

ROVER: Covers the deep half of the field.

FREE SAFETY: Covers the deep half of the field.

STRONG CORNER: Funnels the flanker inside and covers the out.

WEAK CORNER: Funnels the flanker inside and covers the out.

7

Cover 2 Man Stunts

When two-man coverage is employed, both cornerbacks jam the two wide receivers and funnel them to the outside (some coaches may prefer to funnel tightly aligned receivers to the inside). The two safeties use the hashes as landmarks to defend the deep halves of the field. A wide variety of stunt tactics may be employed with this coverage.

Two-Man Techniques for Cornerbacks

A defensive cornerback should:

- Line up so that his inside foot is splitting the receiver's stance.
- Set up with a narrow base, feet parallel, and shoulders square to the line. His weight should be equally balanced on the balls of his feet.
- Focus his concentration on the receiver's midsection.
- Mirror the receiver's release be stepping laterally.
- Jam the receiver with both hands aiming for his pecks. He should not lunge. The defender should lock his elbows and deny the receiver an easy release, but not lose balance by being overly aggressive. He should not allow the receiver to get too close to him, by trying to maintain an arms-length distance.

- Punch the receiver's inside shoulder with his inside hand versus and inside release. He should slide parallel with the receiver and ride him down the line, denying the receiver an inside release.

- Open his hips slightly (without opening the gate) and get his inside hand on the receiver's inside shoulder versus an outside release.

- Trail the receiver at a distance that enables the defender to reach out and touch the receiver's back pocket. If the defender can't touch the receiver, there is too much separation between the two of them, and the cornerback must close the gap. When trailing, the defender should ideally be one yard inside and one yard behind the receiver.

- Maintain inside leverage by keeping his body between the receiver and the ball.

- Concentrate on the receiver's hips and feet as he trails him.

Adjusting Cover 2 Man to Offensive Formations

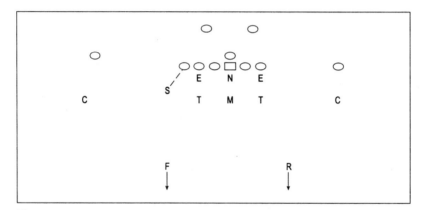

Figure 7-1a

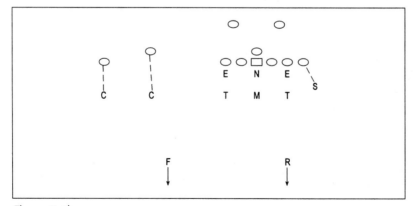

Figure 7-1b

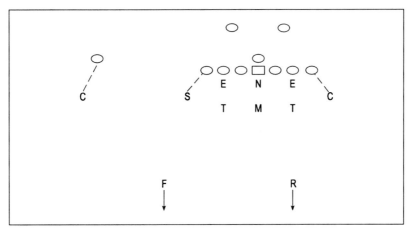

Figure 7-1c

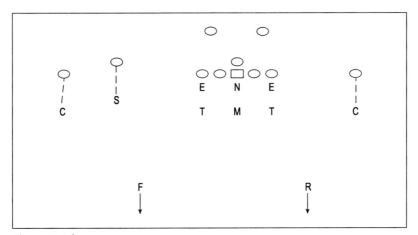

Figure 7-1d

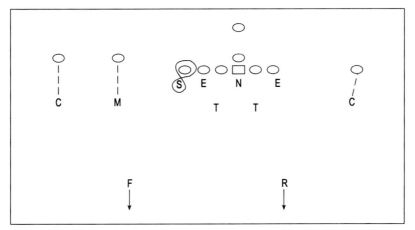

Figure 7-1e

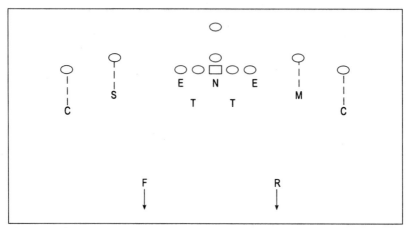

Figure 7-1f

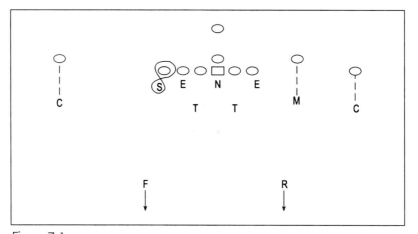

Figure 7-1g

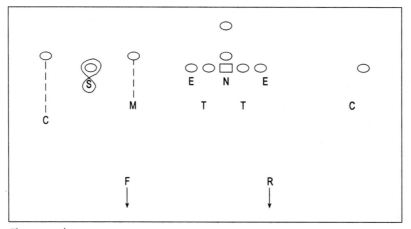

Figure 7-1h

STUNT #84

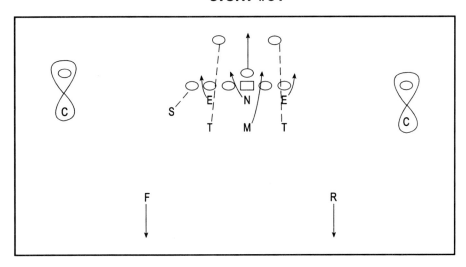

STUNT DESCRIPTION: This *stunt* sends Mike.

SECONDARY COVERAGE: Cover 2 man. The Tandems cover the running backs and the Stud covers the tight end.

STUD: Plays 8 technique versus run. Funnels the tight end inside versus pass.

STRONG END: Slants outside, controls the C gap, and contains the quarterback.

STRONG TANDEM: Plays base technique against run. Covers the near back versus pass.

NOSE: Slants into and controls the strongside A gap.

MIKE: Blitzes through the weakside A gap.

WEAK END: Slants outside, controls the C gap, and contains the quarterback.

WEAK TANDEM: Plays base technique against run. Covers the near back versus pass.

ROVER: Covers the deep half of the field.

FREE SAFETY: Covers the deep half of the field.

STRONG CORNER: Covers the flanker (press technique).

WEAK CORNER: Covers the split end (press technique).

STUNT #85

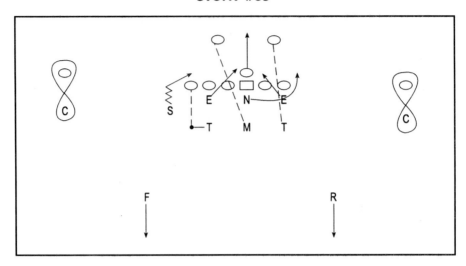

STUNT DESCRIPTION: This *stunt* sends Stud and provides the defense with a weakside line twist.

SECONDARY COVERAGE: Cover 2 man. The Mike and the weak Tandem cover the running backs and the strong Tandem covers the tight end.

STUD: Creeps toward the line of scrimmage during cadence and rushes from the edge. Contains the quarterback and strongside run. Chases weakside run.

STRONG END: Attacks the near shoulder of the offensive guard and controls the B gap.

STRONG TANDEM: Shuffles outside at the snap and covers the tight end (funnels him inside).

NOSE: Loops to the outside shoulder of the offensive tackle, controls the weakside C gap, and contains the quarterback.

MIKE: Plays base technique versus run. Covers the strong back versus pass.

WEAK END: Attacks the near shoulder of the offensive guard and controls the B gap.

WEAK TANDEM: Plays base technique against run. Covers the near back versus pass.

ROVER: Covers the deep half of the field.

FREE SAFETY: Covers the deep half of the field.

STRONG CORNER: Covers the flanker (press technique).

WEAK CORNER: Covers the split end (press technique).

STUNT #86

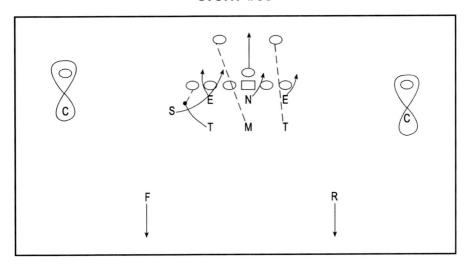

STUNT DESCRIPTION: This *stunt* sends Stud and provides the defense with a weakside line slant.

SECONDARY COVERAGE: Cover 2 man. Mike and the weak Tandem cover the running backs and the strong Tandem covers the tight end.

STUD: Stunts through and controls the strongside B gap at the snap.

STRONG END: Slants outside, controls the C gap, and contains the quarterback.

STRONG TANDEM: Immediately moves to a position that will enable him to procure outside leverage on the tight end. His land mark is the tight end's outside shoulder. Contains strongside run if the tight end blocks and covers him if he releases.

NOSE: Slants into and controls the weakside A gap.

MIKE: Plays base technique versus run. Covers the strong back versus pass.

WEAK END: Slants outside, controls the C gap, and contains the quarterback.

WEAK TANDEM: Plays base technique against run. Covers the near back versus pass.

ROVER: Covers the deep half of the field.

FREE SAFETY: Covers the deep half of the field.

STRONG CORNER: Covers the flanker (press technique).

WEAK CORNER: Covers the split end (press technique).

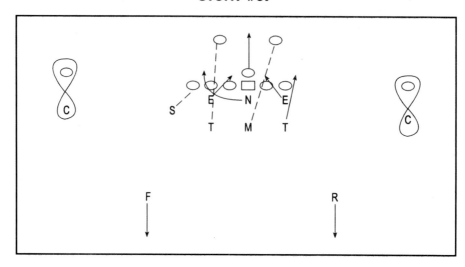

STUNT DESCRIPTION: This *stunt* sends the weak Tandem and provides the defense with a strongside line twist.

SECONDARY COVERAGE: Cover 2 man. Mike and the strong Tandem cover the running backs and Stud covers the tight end.

STUD: Plays 8 technique versus run. Covers the tight end versus pass (funnels him inside).

STRONG END: Attacks the near shoulder of the offensive guard and controls the B gap.

STRONG TANDEM: Plays base technique versus run. Covers the near back versus pass.

NOSE: Loops to the outside shoulder of the offensive tackle, controls the strongside C gap, and contains the quarterback.

MIKE: Plays base technique versus run. Covers the weak back versus pass.

WEAK END: Attacks the near shoulder of the offensive guard and controls the B gap.

WEAK TANDEM: Blitzes through the outside shoulder of the offensive tackle. Controls the C gap and contains the quarterback.

ROVER: Covers the deep half of the field.

FREE SAFETY: Covers the deep half of the field.

STRONG CORNER: Covers the flanker (press technique).

WEAK CORNER: Covers the split end (press technique).

STUNT #88

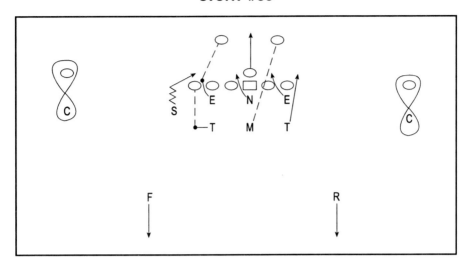

STUNT DESCRIPTION: This *stunt* sends both the Stud and weak Tandem and provides the defense with a strongside line slant.

SECONDARY COVERAGE: Cover 2 man. Mike and the strong end cover the running backs and the strong Tandem covers the tight end.

STUD: Creeps toward the line of scrimmage during cadence and rushes from the edge. Contains the quarterback and strongside run. Chases weakside run.

STRONG END: Slants outside and secures the C gap versus run. Spies the near back versus pass.

STRONG TANDEM: Shuffles outside at the snap and covers the tight end (funnels him inside).

NOSE: Slants into and controls the strongside A gap.

MIKE: Plays base technique versus run. Covers the weak back versus pass.

WEAK END: Attacks the near shoulder of the offensive guard and controls the B gap.

WEAK TANDEM: Blitzes through the outside shoulder of the offensive tackle. Controls the C gap and contains the quarterback.

ROVER: Covers the deep half of the field.

FREE SAFETY: Cover the deep half of the field.

STRONG CORNER: Covers the flanker (press technique).

WEAK CORNER: Covers the split end (press technique).

STUNT #89

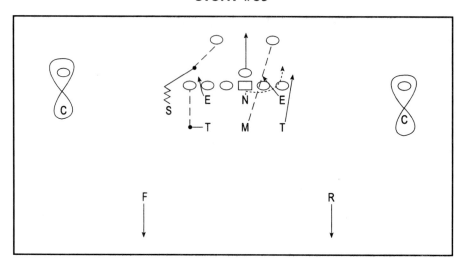

STUNT DESCRIPTION: This *stunt* sends the weak Tandem and provides the defense with a weakside twin stunt.

SECONDARY COVERAGE: Cover 2 man. The Mike and Stud cover the running backs and the strong Tandem covers the tight end.

STUD: Creeps toward the line of scrimmage during cadence and rushes from the edge. Contains strongside run and chases weakside run. Spies the near back versus pass.

STRONG END: Slants outside and controls the C gap.

STRONG TANDEM: Shuffles outside at the snap and covers the tight end (funnels him inside).

NOSE: Plays 0 technique versus run. Slants into the weakside B gap versus pass.

MIKE: Plays base technique versus run. Covers the weak back versus pass.

WEAK END: Slants into and quickly penetrates the B gap.

WEAK TANDEM: Blitzes through the outside shoulder of the offensive tackle. Controls the C gap and contains the quarterback.

ROVER: Covers the deep half of the field.

FREE SAFETY: Covers the deep half of the field.

STRONG CORNER: Covers the flanker (press technique).

WEAK CORNER: Covers the split end (press technique).

8

Adapting 3-5 Stunt Tactics to Aceback and Empty Formations

STUNT #90

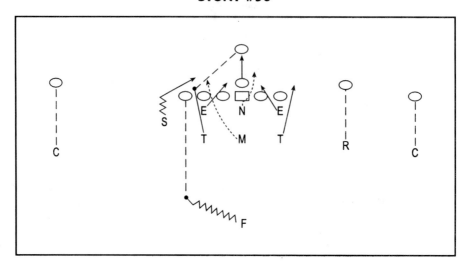

STUNT DESCRIPTION: This is a *blitz* that provides the defense with a strongside overload via a delayed linebacker blitz.

SECONDARY COVERAGE: Zero coverage disguised as cover 1.

STUD: Creeps toward the line of scrimmage during cadence and rushes from the edge. Contains the quarterback and strongside run. Chases weakside run.

STRONG END: Attacks the near shoulder of the offensive guard and controls the B gap.

STRONG TANDEM: Blitzes through the outside shoulder of the offensive tackle and secures the C gap. Spies the near back. He is only responsible for the near back if he blocks strong. Continue to rush through the C gap if he blocks weak.

NOSE: Plays 0 technique versus run. Rushes through the weak A gap versus pass.

MIKE: Plays base technique versus run. Covers the aceback .if he blocks weak versus pass. Blitzes through the strongside A gap if aceback blocks strong

WEAK END: Attacks the near shoulder of the offensive guard and controls the B gap.

WEAK TANDEM: Stunts through the outside shoulder of the offensive tackle and secures the C gap. Contains the quarterback versus pass.

ROVER: Covers #2 weak (inside technique).

FREE SAFETY: Covers the tight end. Disguises his assignment as cover 1.

STRONG CORNER: Covers the flanker (inside technique).

WEAK CORNER: Covers split end (inside technique).

STUNT #91

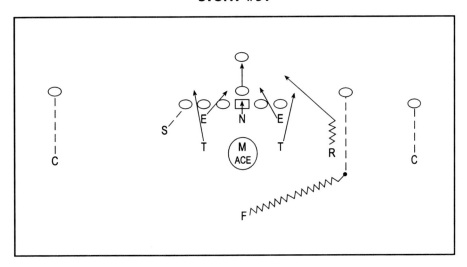

STUNT DESCRIPTION: This blitz frees Mike to back up the defenders penetrating the gaps.

SECONDARY COVERAGE: Zero coverage disguised as cover 1.

STUD: Covers the tight end.

STRONG END: Attacks the near shoulder of the offensive guard and controls the B gap.

STRONG TANDEM: Blitzes through and controls the C gap. Contains the quarterback versus pass.

NOSE: Plays 0 technique.

MIKE: Plays base technique versus run. Covers the aceback versus pass.

WEAK END: Attacks the near shoulder of the offensive guard and controls; the B gap.

WEAK TANDEM: Stunts through the outside shoulder of the offensive tackle. Controls the C gap versus run and contains the quarterback versus pass.

ROVER: Creeps inside during cadence and rushes from the edge. Contains the quarterback and weakside run. Chases strongside run.

FREE SAFETY: Covers receiver #2 weak. Disguises his assignment as cover 1.

STRONG CORNER: Cover the flanker (inside technique).

WEAK CORNER: Covers the split end (inside technique).

STUNT #92

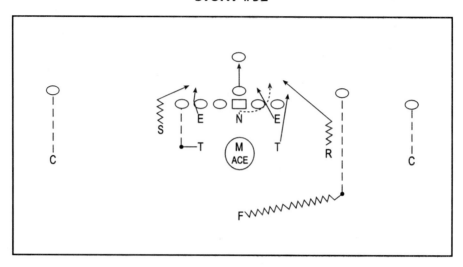

STUNT DESCRIPTION: This *blitz* t frees Mike to back up the defenders penetrating the gaps and provides the defense with a weakside overload via a delayed line twist.

SECONDARY COVERAGE: Zero coverage disguised as cover 1.

STUD: Creeps forward during cadence and rushes from the edge. Contains the quarterback and strongside run. Chases weakside run.

STRONG END: Slants outside and controls the C gap.

STRONG TANDEM: Shuffles outside at the snap and covers the tight end.

NOSE: Plays 0 technique versus run. Loops through the weakside B gap versus pass.

MIKE: Plays base technique versus run. Covers the aceback versus pass.

WEAK END: Attacks the near shoulder of the offensive guard and controls the B gap.

WEAK TANDEM: Stunts through the outside shoulder of the offensive tackle and controls the C gap.

ROVER: Creeps inside during cadence and rushes from the edge. Contains the quarterback and weakside run. Chases strongside run.

FREE SAFETY: Covers receiver #2 weak. Disguises his assignment as cover 1.

STRONG CORNER: Covers the flanker (inside technique).

WEAK CORNER: Covers the split end (inside technique).

STUNT #93

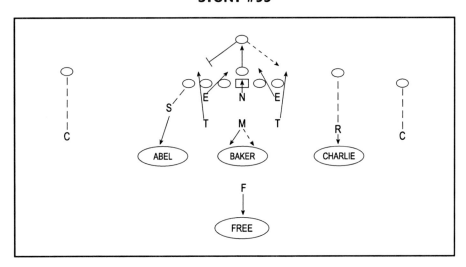

STUNT DESCRIPTION: This is a *fire zone blitz.*

SECONDARY COVERAGE: Cover 1 disguised as cover 3.

STUD: Plays 8 technique versus run. Keys the block of the aceback versus pass. If Ace blocks strong, he combo-covers the aceback and tight end with Mike (**Abel**). If Ace blocks weak, he covers the tight end by himself.

STRONG END: Attacks the near shoulder of the offensive guard and controls the B gap.

STRONG TANDEM: Blitzes through and controls the C gap. Contains the quarterback versus pass.

NOSE: Plays 0 technique.

MIKE: Plays base technique versus run. Drops **Baker** versus pass. Keys the Aceback. If Ace blocks strong, he combo covers the aceback and tight end with Stud. If Ace blocks weak, he combo-covers Ace and receiver #2 weak with Rover.

WEAK END: Attacks the near shoulder of the offensive guard and controls the B gap.

WEAK TANDEM: Stunts through the outside shoulder of the offensive tackle. Controls the C gap versus run and contains the quarterback versus pass.

ROVER: Plays 8 technique versus run. He keys the block of the aceback versus pass. If Ace blocks weak, he combo-covers the aceback and receiver #2 weak with Mike (**Charlie**). If Ace blocks strong, he covers receiver #2 weak by himself.

FREE SAFETY: Lines up as though he's playing cover 3. Provides alley support to run. Plays centerfield versus pass.

STRONG CORNER: Plays cover 1. Inside/outside technique dependent upon field position and the distance of flanker's split.

WEAK CORNER: Plays cover 1. Inside/outside technique dependent upon field position and the distance of split end's split.

STUNT #94

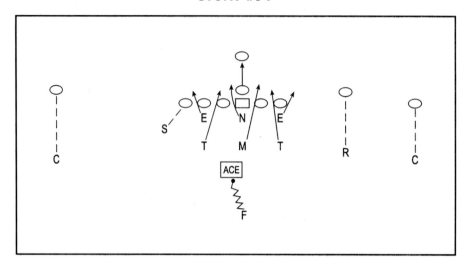

STUNT DESCRIPTION: This is a *blitz* that provides the defense with excellent inside pressure.

SECONDARY COVERAGE: Zero coverage disguised as cover 1.

STUD: Covers the tight end.

STRONG END: Slants outside, controls the C gap, and contains the quarterback.

STRONG TANDEM: Blitzes through the outside shoulder of the offensive guard and controls the B gap.

NOSE: Slants into and controls the strongside A gap.

MIKE: Blitzes through the weakside A gap.

WEAK END: Slants outside, controls the C gap, and contains the quarterback.

WEAK TANDEM: Blitzes through the outside shoulder of the offensive guard and controls the B gap.

ROVER: Covers receiver #2 weak (inside technique).

FREE SAFETY: Disguises his assignment as cover 1. Creeps toward the line of scrimmage during cadence and gives the offense the impression that a safety blitz is in progress. Provides alley support to run and covers the aceback versus pass.

STRONG CORNER: Covers flanker (inside technique).

WEAK CORNER: Covers split end (inside technique).

STUNT #95

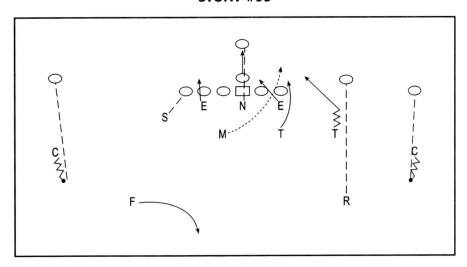

STUNT DESCRIPTION: This *dog* provides the defense with a weakside overload via a *delayed linebacker blitz.*

SECONDARY COVERAGE: Cover 1 disguised as cover 2.

STUD: Plays 8 technique versus run. Covers the tight end versus pass.

STRONG END: Slants outside, controls the C gap, and contains the quarterback.

STRONG TANDEM: Lines up opposite #2 receiver weak, but creeps inside during cadence and rushes from the edge. Contains the quarterback and weakside run. Chases strongside run.

NOSE: Plays 0 technique versus run. Spies the aceback versus pass.

MIKE: Secures the B gap versus strongside run and pursues weakside run from an inside-out position. Blitzes through the weakside B gap versus pass.

WEAK END: Attacks the near shoulder of the offensive guard and controls the B gap.

WEAK TANDEM: Blitzes through the outside shoulder of the offensive tackle and controls the C gap.

ROVER: Lines up as though he's playing cover 2, but covers receiver #2 weak.

FREE SAFETY: Lines up as though he's playing cover 2. Provides alley support to run and drops to centerfield versus pass.

STRONG CORNER: Lines up as though he's playing cover 2. Covers the flanker. Inside/outside technique dependent upon field position and the distance of flanker's split.

WEAK CORNER: Lines up as though he's playing cover 2. Covers the split end. Inside/outside technique dependent upon field position and the distance of split end's split.

STUNT #96

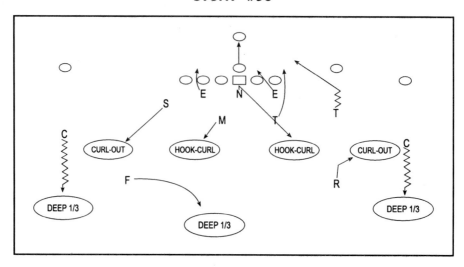

STUNT DESCRIPTION: This is an *old school zone blitz*.

SECONDARY COVERAGE: Cover 3 disguised as cover 2.

STUD: Plays 8 technique versus run. Drops curl-out versus pass.

STRONG END: Slants outside, controls the C gap, and contains the quarterback.

STRONG TANDEM: Lines up opposite receiver #2 weak, but creeps inside during cadence and rushes from the edge. Contains the quarterback and weakside run. Chases strongside run.

NOSE: Plays 0 technique versus run. Drops hook-curl versus pass.

MIKE: Secures the B gap versus strongside run and pursue weakside run from an inside-out position. Drops hook-curl versus pass.

WEAK END: Attacks the near shoulder of the offensive guard and controls the B gap.

WEAK TANDEM: Blitzes through the outside shoulder of the offensive tackle and controls the C gap.

ROVER: Lines up as though he's playing cover 2. Plays 8 technique versus run. Drops curl-out versus pass.

FREE SAFETY: Lines up as though he's playing cover 2. Provides alley support to run and drops to centerfield and covers the deep middle versus pass.

STRONG CORNER: Lines up as though he's playing cover 2, but covers the deep outside third.

WEAK CORNER: Lines up as though he's playing cover 2, but covers the deep outside third.

STUNT #97

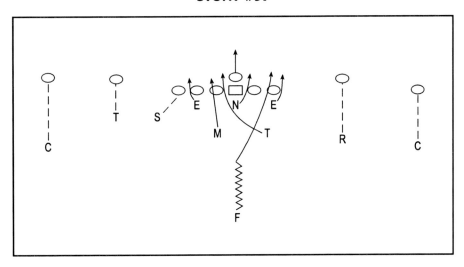

STUNT DESCRIPTION: This is a *blitz* (versus an empty set) that provides the defense with a free safety blitz.

SECONDARY COVERAGE: Zero coverage disguised as Cover 1.

STUD: Covers the tight end.

STRONG END: Slants outside, controls the C gap, and contains the quarterback.

STRONG TANDEM: Covers receiver #2 strong.

NOSE: Slants into and controls the weakside A gap.

MIKE: Blitzes through the outside shoulder of the offensive guard and controls the strongside B gap.

WEAK END: Slants outside, controls the C gap, and contains the quarterback.

WEAK TANDEM: Blitzes through the strongside A gap.

ROVER: Covers receiver #2 weak (inside technique).

FREE SAFETY: Disguises his assignment as cover 1. Creeps toward the line of scrimmage during cadence and blitzes through the weakside B gap.

STRONG CORNER: Covers the flanker (inside technique).

WEAK CORNER: Covers the split end (inside technique).

STUNT #98

STUNT DESCRIPTION: This *blitz* (versus an empty set) provides the defense with excellent inside pressure and a strongside overload via a delayed linebacker blitz.

SECONDARY COVERAGE: Zero coverage disguised as cover 1.

STUD: Plays 8 technique versus run. Blitzes through the strongside A gap versus pass.

STRONG END: Slants outside, controls the C gap, and contains the quarterback.

STRONG TANDEM: Covers receiver #2 strong.

NOSE: Plays O technique versus run. Quickly penetrates the strongside A gap versus pass.

MIKE: Blitzes through the outside shoulder of the offensive guard and controls the strongside B gap.

WEAK END: Slants into and controls the B gap.

WEAK TANDEM: Blitzes through the outside shoulder of the offensive tackle. Controls the C gap and contains the quarterback.

ROVER: Covers receiver #2 weak (inside technique).

FREE SAFETY: Covers the tight end. Disguises his assignment as cover 1.

STRONG CORNER: Covers the flanker (inside technique).

WEAK CORNER: Covers the split end (inside technique).

STUNT #99

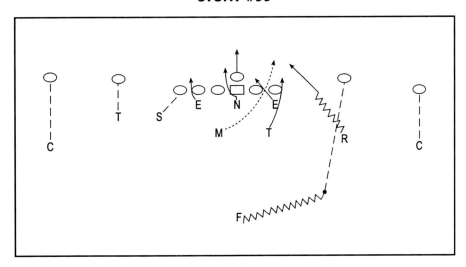

STUNT DESCRIPTION: This *blitz* (versus an empty set) provides the defense with a weakside overload via a delayed linebacker blitz.

SECONDARY COVERAGE: Zero coverage disguised as cover 1.

STUD: Covers the tight end.

STRONG END: Slants outside, controls the C gap, and contains the quarterback.

STRONG TANDEM: Covers receiver #2 strong.

NOSE: Plays O technique versus run. Rushes through the strongside A gap versus pass.

MIKE: Secures the B gap versus strongside run and pursues weakside run from an inside-out position. Blitzes through the weakside B gap versus pass.

WEAK END: Slants into and controls the B gap.

WEAK TANDEM: Blitzes through the outside shoulder of the offensive tackle and controls the C gap.

ROVER: Lines up opposite receiver #2 weak, but creeps inside during cadence and rushes from the edge. Contains the quarterback and weakside run. Chases strongside run.

FREE SAFETY: Covers receiver #2 weak. Disguises his assignment as cover 1.

STRONG CORNER: Covers the flanker (inside technique).

WEAK CORNER: Covers the split end (inside technique).

STUNT #100

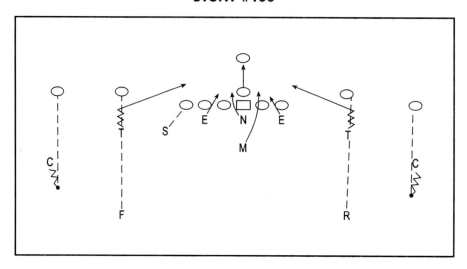

STUNT DESCRIPTION: This blitz (versus an empty set) provides the defense with excellent outside pressure.

SECONDARY COVERAGE: Zero coverage disguised as over 2.

STUD: Covers the tight end.

STRONG END: Slants into controls the B gap.

STRONG TANDEM: Lines up as though he intends to cover receiver #2 strong, but creeps inside during cadence and rushes from the edge. Contains the quarterback and strongside run. Chases weakside run.

NOSE: Quickly penetrates the strongside A gap.

MIKE: Blitzes through the weakside A gap.

WEAK END: Slants into and controls the B gap.

WEAK TANDEM: Lines up as though he intends to cover receiver #2 weak, but creeps inside during cadence and rushes from the edge. Contains the quarterback and weakside run. Chases strongside run.

ROVER: Covers receiver #2 weak. Disguises his assignment as cover 2.

FREE SAFETY: Covers receiver #2 strong. Disguises his assignment as cover 2.

STRONG CORNER: Covers the flanker (inside technique). Disguises his assignment as cover 2.

WEAK CORNER: Covers the split end (inside technique). Disguises his assignment as cover 2.

STUNT #101

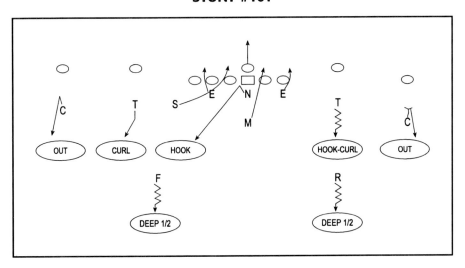

STUNT DESCRIPTION: This is an *old school zone blitz*.

SECONDARY COVERAGE: Cover 2.

STUD: Blitzes through the strongside B gap.

STRONG END: Slants outside, controls the C gap, and contains the quarterback.

STRONG TANDEM: Plays 8 technique versus run. Drops curl versus pass.

NOSE: Slants to and controls the strongside A gap versus run. Drops hook versus pass.

MIKE: Blitzes through the weakside A gap.

WEAK END: Slants outside, controls the C gap, and contains the quarterback.

WEAK TANDEM: Plays 8 technique versus run. Drops hook-curl versus pass.

ROVER: Covers the deep half of the field.

FREE SAFETY: Covers the deep half of the field.

STRONG CORNER: Funnels the flanker inside and covers the out.

WEAK CORNER: Funnels the flanker inside and covers the out.

9

Defending the Option with the 3-5 Defense

The 3-5 defense is one of football's best option defenses. When playing an option team, it is best to move the defensive ends to a loose five technique and align the tandems five yards deep on the inside eye of the offensive tackles. From this alignment, the ends and tandems will be able to read the block of the offensive tackle and adjust their option assignments accordingly (coaches refer to this as a *tango* read).

Another coaching point that should be mentioned when discussing option defense is that the defense must not allow the offensive center and backside guard to zone block (scoop block) the nose and mike. If the offense is able to execute this blocking scheme, the defense will have a difficult time stopping them.

Stopping the Inside Veer

There are two schemes that an offense may employ to run an inside veer. The first scheme is illustrated in Figure 9-1.

The assignments the five flowside defenders employ versus this inside veer blocking scheme follow:

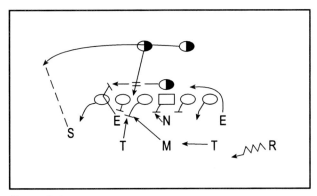

Figure 9-1

Stud:

- Attacks the tight end's outside shoulder to take away the quick dump pass
- Prepares to defeat the tight end's block. If the tight end attempts to block, he penetrates the backfield and immediately goes to the pitch.
- If the tight end is arc releasing to block the free safety, he feathers the pitch. He disguises the technique by making it appear that he's playing the quarterback.
- Maintains a depth of two to three yards from the line of scrimmage and never wider than one yard from the quarterback.
- Strings the play to the sidelines.
- Be cognizant of the pitchback. Immediately plays the pitchback if he gets even with him.
- When feathering the quarterback he opens up his inside foot and attacks the quarterback's pitch arm should he turn upfield. If, the quarterback pitches the ball, he breaks at a 45-degree angle (to the line of scrimmage) and tackles the pitchback.

End:

- Reads the tackle's head. As the tackle turns to block him, he quickly penetrates the C gap and attacks the quarterback's pitch arm.

Tandem:

- Reads the tackle's block. As he sees the tackle block the end, he immediately fills the B gap.
- Defeats the guard's block with an inside forearm rip and tackles the diveback.

Nose:

- Prevents the center from releasing to the next level. Plugs the A gap and plays cutback.

Mike:

- He should be left unblocked. Plays dive-quarterback. If there is any doubt, punishes the dive back.

The assignments the five flow side defenders employ versus this inside veer blocking scheme are as follows:

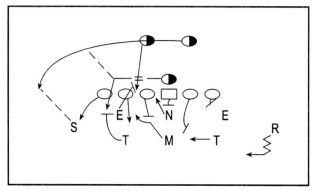

Figure 9-2

Stud:

- Same as previous scheme.

End:

- Jams the tackle with his inside hand and quickly gains penetration. Attacks the diveback at the mesh and forces the quarterback to run the play *downhill*.

Tandem:

- Scrapes to the C gap. Avoids the tackle's block. Tackles the quarterback.

Nose:

- Defeats the center's block and plugs the A gap. Tackles the diveback from an inside-out position.

Mike:

- Rips through the guard's outside shoulder with his far arm. Plays dive-quarterback.
- If in doubt, tackles the fullback dive.

These defensive tactics are necessary to stop the inside veer when it is run toward the split end. They are also effective versus the inside veer toward the tight end. There is, however an alternative method that can be used to stop the inside veer toward the tight end, and it can be used whenever the offense employs a standard pro set formation. This method involves assigning the end, the strong tandem, mike and the nose the diveback. Stud is assigned the quarterback, and the free safety and rover employ an inverted rotating secondary and take the pitch man (Figure 9-3). When using this alternative method it is better to play the stud on the line.

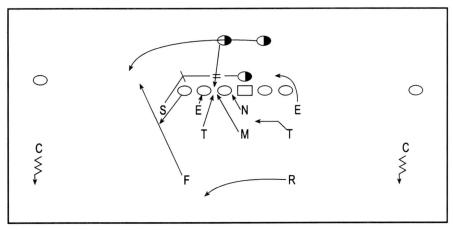

Figure 9-3

Stopping the Outside Veer

There are a number of alignments that can be used to effectively defense the outside veer. One alignment is to position the stud on the line of scrimmage and have him rush from the edge attacking the quarterback at the mesh point. This will force the play inside and enable either the end or strong tandem to tackle the dive in the C gap. When this method is used, the free safety must immediately play the pitch. Obviously, this method is compatible with the inverted, rotating secondary. (Figure 9-4)

Another alignment involves having the stud play a 9 technique and jam the tight end as he attempts the doubleteam. As he jams the tight end, the stud gives the strong tandem a *"down-down"* call which will alert the strong tandem to play the quarterback (similar to the tango technique). This technique is illustrated in Figure 9-5.

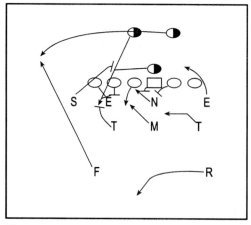

Figure 9-4

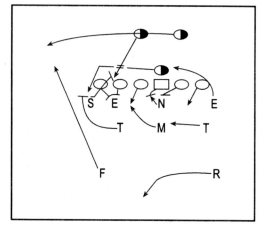

Figure 9-5

Stopping Other Options

Because of it's alignment, most teams do not attempt to run the midline option against the 3-5. Teams will attempt to run the speed (lead) option against the 3-5, but they are seldom successful because there are too many linebackers available to pursue the play. Figure 9-6 illustrates how the 3-5 would react to the speed option.

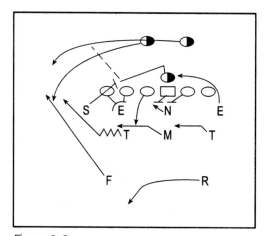

Figure 9-6

10

A Synopsis of D-Line/Linebacker Base Responsibilities

Nose-0 Technique

Stance & Alignment

- Player takes a 3- or 4- point stance, minimum-no stagger, and plays zero technique.

Responsibilities

- *Running play toward player*: Plays play side A gap.
- *Passing play*: Rushes either A gap.

Keys

- *Primary*: Center/ball movement.
- *Secondary*: Both guards.

Important Techniques/Concepts

- Target is the center's facemask.

- *Crush technique*: Player attacks the center with hands—inside lockout. He takes short jab step in direction of play. He controls both A gaps. Player keeps his shoulders square and remembers that the pulling guards indicate point of attack.

Key Blocks

- *Drive block*: Player knocks center back. He stays square, and tries to locate the ball.

- *Double team*: Player attacks guard. He stays low, and must not get driven back.

- *Hook block*: Player controls center's outside shoulder. He keeps his shoulders parallel.

- *Zone block*: Player plays it like a hook block. He keeps center off of the linebacker.

- *Center blocks away/down block by guard*: Player releases from the center and controls the outside shoulder of the guard.

- *Pass*: Player rushes either A gap.

Nose-Slant Technique

Responsibilities

- *Running play towards player*: Plays A gap in direction of his slant.

- *Passing play*: Rushes A gap in direction of his slant.

Keys

- *Primary*: Ball movement/guard in direction of his slant.

- *Secondary*: Center

Important Techniques/Concepts

- Player takes lead step with near foot and then brings back foot through to avoid center's block. Rips backside forearm through with movement of back foot.

- Penetrates with inside hip almost perpendicular to line. Squares up quickly and is ready to move in either direction.

Key Blocks

- *Center blocks the player*: Rip through center's head, turn center's shoulders, and controls A gap. If play is toward his slant, flatten out and go to the ball. If play is away from his slant and he's gained penetration, go around center. If he hasn't gained penetration, come across center's face.

- *Center/Guard zone block away from the slant*: Player ricochets off guard's block and flattens back in opposite direction.
- *Center/Guard zone block toward the slant*: Player rips through center's head. Prevents center from releasing to next level. Avoids guard's block. Plugs A gap.
- *Guard pulls in direction of the slant*: Player rips through center's head and follows guard to point of attack.
- *Guard pulls in opposite direction of the slant*: The center will attempt to block player. If the player gained penetration, go behind the center. If he hasn't gained penetration, comes across the center's face.
- *Guard/Center double team toward the slant*: Attacks guard and tries to flatten across his face. He can't get driven back.
- *Guard/Center double team away from the slant*: Works for penetration and tries to go behind center's block.

Ends–4 Technique

Stance & Alignment

- Player takes a 3- or 4-point stance, minimum-no stagger, and plays 4 technique.

Outside Slant Technique

Responsibilities

- *Running play toward player*: Plays the C gap.
- *Passing play*: Contains the quarterback if stud is involved in coverage.

Keys

- *Primary*: Tackle.
- *Secondary*: Tight end/near back.

Important /Techniques/Concepts

- Player lead steps with near foot and brings back foot through to avoid tackle's block. Rips backside forearm through with movement of back foot.

- Penetrates with inside hip almost perpendicular to line. Squares up quickly and is ready to move in either direction. Anticipates tight end's block if aligned on strongside and near back's block if aligned on weakside.

Key Blocks

- Tackle drive blocks: Player rips through the tackle's head, turns the tackle's shoulders, and controls C gap. If the play is toward his slant, the player flattens out and goes to the ball. If the play is away from his slant and he has gained penetration, he goes behind the tackle. If he hasn't gained penetration, he comes across the tackle's face.
- *Tackle/Guard zone away from the slant*: Player gains quick penetration and flattens back in opposite direction.
- *Tackle/Guard zone toward the slant*: Player rips through tackle's head. Prevents tackle from releasing to next level. Avoids guard's block. Plugs C gap and bounces play outside.
- *Tackle/End double team*: Player attacks tight end and tries to flatten across his face. Player can't get driven back.
- *Tackle blocks inside player left unblocked*: Player stops immediately and flattens back in opposite direction. The point of attack is either away, or he's being trapped. If point of attack is away, he chases as deep as ball. If trapped, the player traps the trapper with his outside arm and bounces the play outside.

Inside Slant Technique

Responsibilities

- *Running play toward player*: Plays B gap.
- *Passing Play*: Penetrates and rushes through B gap.

Keys

- *Primary*: Guard.
- *Secondary*: Tackle.

Important /Techniques/Concepts

- Player lead steps with near foot and then brings back foot through to avoid tackle's block. Rips backside forearm through with movement of back foot.

- Penetrates with inside hip almost perpendicular to line. Squares up quickly and is ready to move in either direction.

Key Blocks

- *Tackle drive blocks and Guard scoops nose*: Player rips through tackle's head, turns tackle's shoulders, and controls B gap. Flattens and goes to the ball.
- *Tackle/Guard zone away from the slant*: Ricochets off guard's block and flattens back in opposite direction.
- *Tackle/Guard zone toward the Slant*: Rips through tackle's head and quickly penetrates B gap.
- *Guard pulls inside-Tackle tries to cut player off*: Player rips through tackle's head and follows guard to point of attack.
- *Guard blocks inside-player left unblocked*: The play is a trap. Player traps the trapper with his outside arm and bounces the play outside.

Stud and Rover-8 Technique

Stance & Alignment

- Player takes a 2 point stance inside foot up, and plays 8 technique.

Responsibilities

- *Running play toward player*: Player comes up quickly and secures D gap.
- *Running play away from player*: Checks tight end first and then pursues the ball.
- *Passing play*: Depends upon coverage.

Keys

- *Primary*: Tight end (if there is one), ball movement.
- *Secondary*: Near back, pulling linemen.

Important Techniques

- Reads tight end's block. Contains run if tight end blocks. Drops into pass coverage if tight end releases.

Key Blocks

- *Tight End blocks inside/near back kicks out*: Off-tackle play. Player fills tight to tight end's block. Seals off any inside seams. Attacks blocker with inside forearm. Spills play outside.

- *Tight end blocks inside/near back hook block*: Sweep. Keeps shoulders parallel to line of scrimmage. Maintains outside leverage. Forces ball carrier inside or wide and deep.

- *Tight end blocks player or releases/near back kicks Out tandem*: Off tackle or play action. If tight end release the player covers him or designated zone. If tight end blocks him, player–squeezes the play inside, while maintaining outside leverage. Player must expect the ball carrier to break the play outside.

- *Tight end blocks player/sweep*: Player must beat tight end's block and blow-up play in the backfield!

- *Tight end releases/flow away*: Player checks tight end for throwback and then pursues.

- *Tight end releases–near back pass blocks: Pass*: Player covers tight end or releases to designated zone.

Mike–Deep 0 Technique

Stance & Alignment

- Player takes a 2-point stance, feet parallel, and stacks three to five yards deep behind the nose.

Responsibilities

- *Running play toward player*: Player comes up quickly and plugs the B gap.
- *Passing play*: Depends upon coverage.

Keys

- *Primary*: Backfield flow.
- *Secondary*: Pulling guards (these take precedence).

Important Techniques

- Player keeps his shoulders parallel to the line of scrimmage. He attacks blocks as close to the line as possible taking on blocker's outside shoulder with his outside leg back. He pursues runs from an inside-out position.

Key Blocks

- *Flow side guard blocks player*: Player attacks guard's outside shoulder as close to line of scrimmage as possible. Maintains outside leverage and bounces play outside. Pursues from an Inside out position.

- *Flow side guard pulls opposite flow*: Player immediately reverses his direction and plugs opposite B gap.

- *Flow side tackle blocks player*: Player controls tackle's outside shoulder and fills outside of his block.

- *Flow side guard blocks inside/near back blocks player: Iso*. Player attacks backs outside shoulder with an inside forearm rip as close to line of scrimmage as possible. Maintains outside leverage and spills the play outside.

- *Passing play*: Depends upon coverage.

Tandems–Deep 4 Technique

Stance & Alignment

- Player take a 2-point stance, feet parallel, and stacks behind the ends three to five yards deep.

Responsibilities

- *Running play toward player*: Player plugs the B or C gap depending on offensive tackle's block and direction of end's slant.

- *Passing play*: Depends upon coverage.

Keys

- *Primary*: Tackle.
- *Secondary*: Backfield flow/pulling guards.

Important Techniques

- Player keeps his shoulders parallel to the line and attacks blocks as close to the line of scrimmage as possible. Attacks blocker's outside shoulder with his outside leg back. Pursues runs from an inside-out position.

Key Blocks

- *End slants outside/tackle blocks end*: Player fills the B gap. Attacks the guard or near back as close to line of scrimmage as possible. He maintains outside leverage, bounces play outside and pursues from an inside out position.

- *End slants outside/tackle blocks player*: If flow is away, player rips through tackles block with outside forearm and pursues ball from an inside-out position. He looks for cutback. If flow is toward the player, he avoids tackle's block and fills the C gap off end's tail (the end should be squeezing the B gap).
- *End slants outside/tackle blocks mike*: Trap! Player fills the B gap.
- *End slants inside/ tackle blocks end*: Player reads flow. If flow is away, he pursues from an inside out position checking for cutback. If flow is toward him, he immediately fills the C gap.
- *End slants inside/tackle blocks player*: Player fills the C gap. He attacks the tackle as close to the line of scrimmage as possible. He maintains outside leverage, bounces play outside and pursues from an inside out position.
- *End slants inside/tackle blocks mike*: Trap! Player fills tight to end's tail.
- *Tight end/tackle double team end*: Player fills close to double team. He takes on near back or pulling lineman with inside forearm. He maintains outside leverage and bounces play outside.
- *Tight end blocks player*: Player attacks tight end with outside forearm. He maintains inside leverage and protects the C gap.
- *Passing play*: Depends upon coverage.

About the Author

Leo Hand is the defensive coordinator at El Paso (TX) High School, a position he assumed in 2001. Prior to that, he held the same job at Irvin High School in El Paso, Texas. With over 33 years of experience as a teacher and coach, Hand has served in a variety of coaching positions in his career. At each stop, he has achieved a notable level of success.

A graduate of Emporia State University in Emporia, Kansas, Hand began his football coaching career in 1968 as the junior varsity coach at McQuaid Jesuit High School in Rochester, New York. After two seasons, he then accepted the job as the offensive line coach at Aquinas Institute (1970-'71). Next, he served as the head coach at Saint John Fisher College—a position he held for two years. He has also served on the gridiron staffs at APW (Parrish, NY) High School (head coach); Saint Anthony (Long Beach, CA) High School (head coach), Daniel Murphy (Los Angeles, CA) High School (head coach), Servite (Anaheim, CA) High School (head coach); Serra (Gardena, CA) High School (head coach); Long Beach (CA) City College (offensive line and linebackers); and Los Angeles (CA) Harbor College (offensive coordinator).

During the last six years that he spent coaching interscholastic teams in California, Hand's squads won 81 percent of their games in the highly competitive area of Southern California. At Serra High School, his teams compiled a 24-1 record, won a CIF championship, and were declared California State champions. On numerous occasions, he has helped rebuild several floundering gridiron teams into highly successful programs. For his efforts, he has been honored on numerous occasions with Coach-of-the-Year recognition.

A former Golden Gloves boxing champion, Hand is a prolific author, having written several football instructional books and numerous articles that have been published. He and his wife, Mary, have nine children and seven grandchildren.